▶ American Politics in the Age of Ignorance

DOI: 10.1057/9781137308733

Other Palgrave Pivot titles

DOI: 10.1057/9781137308733

palgrave▸pivot

American Politics in the Age of Ignorance: Why Lawmakers Choose Belief over Research

David Schultz

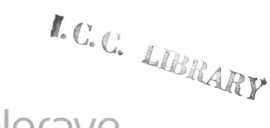

palgrave
macmillan

DOI: 10.1057/9781137308733

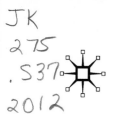

AMERICAN POLITICS IN THE AGE OF IGNORANCE
Copyright © David Schultz, 2013.

First published in 2013 by
PALGRAVE MACMILLAN®
in the United States—a division of St. Martin's Press LLC,
175 Fifth Avenue, New York, NY 10010.

Where this book is distributed in the UK, Europe and the rest of the world,
this is by Palgrave Macmillan, a division of Macmillan Publishers Limited,
registered in England, company number 785998, of Houndmills,
Basingstoke, Hampshire RG21 6XS.

Palgrave Macmillan is the global academic imprint of the above companies
and has companies and representatives throughout the world.

Palgrave® and Macmillan® are registered trademarks in the United States,
the United Kingdom, Europe and other countries.

ISBN: 978–1–137–30872–6 EPUB
ISBN: 978–1–137–30873–3 PDF
ISBN: 978–1–137–30871–9 Hardback

Library of Congress Cataloging-in-Publication Data is available from the
Library of Congress.

A catalogue record of the book is available from the British Library.

First edition: 2013

www.palgrave.com/pivot

DOI: 10.1057/9781137308733

Contents

List of Figures

▶

DOI: 10.1057/9781137308733

Introduction: If at First You Don't Succeed...

Abstract: *Theories about democracy including that in the United States stipulate the necessity for an informed electorate. Additionally it is also assumed that policy makers are well versed about the subjects they address. Unfortunately studies suggest that many American citizens and public officials are woefully ignorant about many facts critical to making informed decisions. The result is that often times many policies and ideas get enacted either when there is little evidence supporting their likelihood of success, or worse, when social science research indicates probable failure. Instead of policy being fact-based, it is often developed in light of political myths that doom the political process to repeated enactment of failed public policies.*

Keywords: Failed policies, political myths, social science evidence, policy making, citizens, democracy, knowledge

Schultz, David. *American Politics in the Age of Ignorance: Why Lawmakers Choose Belief over Research*. New York: Palgrave Macmillan, 2013. DOI: 10.1057/9781137308733.

Elections portend opportunities for change. The change often involves both people and policy. Unfortunately, despite the changes in leadership many of the policies proposed, adopted, and implemented are not new and they will fail. This is not for lack of knowledge about their likely impact. Instead, often ideas or public policies are proposed despite the fact that the best evidence indicates that they will be unsuccessful and ultimately fail. Unmasking some of these proven failures and explaining why American politics seems condemned to enact them is the goal of this book.

Elections are ripe with promise. This was never so apparent as in 2008 when Barack Obama ran for president of the United States with the slogan of "Change" or "Change you can believe in." His narrative of change was embraced by Democrats across the country, catapulting them to secure significant majorities in Congress. The people who voted for him expected new policy directions, including perhaps adoption of a health care reform, new climate legislation, green energy, equal rights for same-sex couples, and perhaps other changes. Yet two years later the Republican Party too ran under the banner of change—this time a change from the policies of Barack Obama—and they successfully took control of the House of Representatives, narrowed the Democratic majority in the Senate, and regained control of many state legislatures and governorships. Their supporters, among them the rising TEA party, too assumed that change meant new policies, such as tax cuts to promote economic growth, cutting back the size of the federal government, and reducing the federal deficit. All this was in addition to a repeal of the reforms enacted by Obama and the Democrats. "Change" as the word of the day dominated these two American elections.

The 2012 as well as future American elections will also bring demands for change. But beyond the sloganeering that accompanies all campaigns, elections are supposed, in part, to be about real change. They reflect the election of new public officials, or reaffirmation of incumbents with new mandates. Elections offer the possibility also of new policies and solutions to old or existing problems. For 2012, the problems at the national level ranged from the economy to health care, taxes, government spending, abortion, gay rights, and a host of other issues. The 50 states will confront issues similar to those found at the federal level, as well as ones that they share. Even at the local level, elections are about change of people and policies. As political scientist E.E. Schattschneider once pointed out, American politics is about the manipulation of the scope of conflict (1960). Some issues may be fought at the local, state, or federal

DOI: 10.1057/9781137308733

levels contingent upon the ability of the winners and losers to socialize or control where political battles may be fought.

The point here simply is to demonstrate that elections in the United States do matter because ultimately they are about public policy. Elections are supposed to signal directions regarding what type of laws or policies should be enacted to solve the pressing issues of the day. The 2008 presidential elections were supposed to be about enacting new ideas that make a difference; the same can be said about 2012 and beyond. Yet when looking at elections and the ideas they produce, three questions surface. The first is about how new are these ideas. By that, candidates and parties often claim that their ideas are new or revolutionary, but are they really? For Mitt Romney and Republicans running in 2012, are tax cuts to stimulate the economy really a new idea? Are claims or demands to get tough on immigration because immigrants are supposed to be a drain on the economy really new? Similarly, at state and local levels, candidates and politicians will contend that tax cuts are needed for economic development, that the building of convention centers are great tools to spur job development, or in some cases, opponents of sex education will argue that teaching it in school encourages sexual promiscuity among adolescents. These are claims and ideas that are not new but have been around for some time. Perhaps sadly, many of the ideas to be proposed in the 2012 and future election cycles have been around for a while, recycled yet again in the political arena because they attract audiences, voters, and cash. These ideas are recycled because they sell. Less cynically they may be resuscitated because people genuinely believe in them and they are important to them.

But whether an idea is new or not, their articulation raises a second important question—will it work? Are tax cuts effective tools to stimulate the economy and produce jobs? Are illegal or undocumented aliens financial drains on, or threats to the economy? Is voter fraud real and are election results altered because of it? Does the building of convention centers and sports stadiums help local economies, and what evidence do we have that the teaching of sex education to teenagers makes them more sexually active? There are a host of ideas that people hold and believe, ideas that are espoused by candidates, but one of the questions is whether they actually have any evidence of their efficacy or truth. Sadly, it often appears that politicians mouth political myths or urban legends that lack evidence of their efficacy. Sometimes they get away with espousing these ideas; other times it dooms them.

DOI: 10.1057/9781137308733

Think about Congresswoman Michele Bachmann's 2012 presidential candidacy. After a first place victory in the August 2011 Iowa straw poll, she was on top of the world. Yet she suddenly fell from political grace. Yes the entrance of Texas Governor Rick Perry hurt her campaign by carving into her political base, but it was also her comments about vaccines that doomed her. In a September 12, 2011 presidential debate Bachmann criticized Perry for an executive order he issued mandating that all sixth-grade girls be vaccinated against the human papillomavirus (HPV) as a measure to prevent cervical cancer. One of Bachmann's criticisms was that such an order was an overreach of government authority and an infringement upon individual liberty. This is a fair argument. But she continued her attack the next day on the NBC's Today show. Describing her conversation with a woman after the debate, Bachmann recounted: "She told me that her little daughter took that vaccine, that injection, and she suffered from mental retardation thereafter. There is no second chance for these little girls if there is [sic] any dangerous consequences to their bodies" (ABC News 2011).

Bachmann's repeating of the urban legend that vaccines cause cognitive problems—retardation—was swiftly condemned by the medical community. The source of this claim was a long discredited and doctored study that purported to find this link. The medical evidence was significant—there was no connection and instead one could argue, as Governor Perry had correctly suggested in the debate, that HPV and other vaccines would be medically beneficial and would better promote public health than not getting the vaccine. Yet because of this urban legend connecting vaccines with autism, parents were refusing to inoculate their children.

Bachmann's repeated and apparent embrace of this myth was roundly criticized. Suddenly she looked like some type of crackpot, ready to embrace outlandish and fringe ideas. Some might have concluded that Michele Bachmann believes the world is flat, the Earth is at the center of a universe God created on the evening of Sunday, October 23, 4004 BC (according to calculations by Medieval Bishop James Ussher), and that Elvis is still alive and well and living in hiding somewhere, thereby explaining why she wished him happy birthday on the anniversary of his alleged death.

Bachmann boiled a cauldron of fringe views and crank beliefs. But it is not simply her; American politics seems unable to incorporate evidence and research into its public policy, including in areas such as health care

DOI: 10.1057/9781137308733

and medical treatment (*Economist* 2012). Additionally it appears that many members of the Republican Party, especially but not exclusively the Tea Party wing, seem to reject science and evidence (Mooney 2012; Mooney 2006). The Republican Party is in danger of being sucked back into the Dark Ages, rejecting science and learning in favor of crackpot ideas that are the currency of conspiracists and Medievalists who fear the world is changing and they are unwilling to accept it. But truth and science did not seem to matter to Bachmann and the Republican presidential field during 2011–2012—they instead seem to wear their ignorance and prejudice well—and it appeals to the voters they are courting.

Bachmann saw the floods and earthquakes in Washington, D.C. in 2011 as a sign from God. She came out against the belief in global warming as did Rick Perry and many other Republicans. Many still question evolution, and in states such as Kansas conservatives still seek to ban it from school or require creation science to be taught next to it. They believe that the teaching of sex education in schools promotes promiscuity, talking about how homosexuality causes kids to become gay, and that conservation efforts to ban incandescent light bulbs are a fundamental interference with the right to liberty. And Ron Paul opined for a return to the gold standard. One waited in the 2012 presidential debates for someone to come out against fluoridation of water because it turns us into communists, that a second shooter existed on the grassy knoll in Dallas in 1963, and that the CIA is suppressing evidence of the presence of space aliens in New Mexico area 51. At least no one proposed a return to leeches and blood-letting as an alternative to Obamacare! All these positions are myths, urban legends, and beliefs held by a growing anti-intellectual bloc within American society and which seemed poised to take over the Republican Party.

American historian Richard Hofstadter once wrote about a paranoid style to American politics that resented intellectualism and leaning (2008). It is a dark side of American politics, connecting the Salem witch hunts to the Alien and Sedition Acts of 1798, the Know Nothing Party of the nineteenth century, McCarthyism in the 1950s, and the new isolationism and Arab-Muslim fears in a post-9/11 world. It oozes fear of science and rationalism, dislikes government authority—but only if it supports causes deemed Anti-American—and it targets those who dare to criticize the United States.

This anti-intellectualism explains current demands for voter IDs, finding the reason why Democrats win is because those people—felons,

DOI: 10.1057/9781137308733

immigrants, young people, and minorities—fraudulently voted, and it also accounts for the hatred of Obama's appeal to reason and intellect. Such anti-intellectualism informs policy making and its opposition to Keynesianism, support for supply-economics, and the preternatural belief that tax cuts are the cure for everything except with it comes to Obama's job proposals. It is an incoherent set of beliefs searching for the founders' intent in interpreting the Constitution, looking for a literalism in the document that parallels the type found in the Bible and refuted by Clarence Darrow in the famous 1925 Scope Trial. It is a rejection not just of science, but of any facts and social science that can guide policy making.

What is worse? Is it that there is a segment of the American population that continues to embrace all these crank ideas, or that major candidates for the Republican presidential nomination are pandering to these beliefs? There is a danger to this for the Republicans. Governor John Huntsmann perhaps captured it well at the September 2011 Reagan Library presidential debate: "Listen, when you make comments that fly in the face of what 98 out of 100 climate scientists have said, when you call into question the science of evolution, all I'm saying is that, in order for the Republican Party to win, we can't run from science" (History Musings 2011).

Huntsmann's comment slammed what Tim Blotz (2011) described as Bachmann's "belief-based politics." It is a politics that ignores science—not just the hard sciences such as chemistry or biology—but also the social sciences of economics and political science. Bachmann's comments about the HPV do not stand in isolation. She was often criticized for factual inaccuracies in many claims, ranging from assertions that the American constitutional framers freed the slaves (they did not) to the claim that Dodd–Frank Act (the bill passed in 2010 to regulate Wall Street financial transactions) and the Patient Protection and Affordable Care Act (Obamacare) have already led to the loss of millions of American jobs or increased health care costs despite the fact that most of the major provisions of both had yet to go into effect. She also simply and repeatedly made other assertions that were simply wrong or widely exaggerated. Louis Jacobson of Politifact points out that Bachmann, through 2010, has earned five "Pants on Fire" ratings on the Truth-O-Meter and has never scored better than "false" in her five truth tests (Jacobson 2010).

Republicans do not have a monopoly on embracing failed ideas or espousing myths. Some Democrats claim President George Bush deliberately lied about weapons of mass destruction in Iraq as a pretext for starting a war. Some also share in myths about immigrants as economic drains on the economy, or spend significant resources on sports stadium or convention hall construction in the belief they will be significant economic stimuli for local economies. All of these beliefs speak to a significant paradox in American politics. Often ideas are proposed by politicians or elected officials but they are untested or unproven regarding their efficacy or viability. Yes there are times when experimentation is needed and worthy. Franklin Roosevelt and the policies he proposed to rescue the country from the Depression of the 1930s involved risk-taking and taking chances. Alice Rivlin, former director of the Congressional Budget Office and also the Office of Management and Budget, writes in her 1971 classic *Systematic Thinking for Social Action* of the need to do more experimentation in the policy making and implementation process to determine what works or not. Such experimentation, including pilot projects often can yield important information that can lead to true policy innovation and success. For some, experiments under the Nixon administration to test the earned income tax credit yielded important information about the Earned Income Tax Credits program and how it could be a successful anti-poverty pro-work program. Based on its testing in New Jersey it was expanded and it remains a hallmark of a successful program to this day.

Today there is even more emphasis on stretching the public dollars than ever before. The American public wants money to be spent well, for programs that work. We abhor waste and fraud. In schools of public policy emphasis is placed upon teaching best practices and on results-orientated programs. Obama has said many times that if government programs do not work they should be scrapped. The demand to do more with less drives the demand for efficiency and results.

But with all the emphasis on doing what works, what we know is often ignored. Why? Initially, two arguments can be made. First, the American public is woefully ignorant about American politics and government, and second, the same may be true for many elected representatives when it comes to understanding social and hard science information. Consider first the American public.

Rick Shenkman's *Just How Stupid Are We? Facing the Truth About the American Voter* describes the declining literacy in American politics (2009). He notes how at a time when Americans seem to be demanding more and more opportunity to engage in direct democracy via initiative

DOI: 10.1057/9781137308733

and referendum, they seem to know even less and less about basic facts regarding how the political process works. Similarly, in perhaps the most comprehensive study on American political literacy Michael DelliCarpini and Scott Keeter confirm the public's ignorance in *What Americans Don't Know About Politics and Why It Matters* (1989). Drawing upon extensive survey research, they found barely 40% could define the Bill of Rights, over 40% did not know that the Supreme Court could declare laws unconstitutional, only 20% could name two first Amendment rights, and only 19% could name all three branches of the national government (DelliCarpini and Keeter 1989: 70–71). Survey research in general suggests that only 59% of the population according to a Pew study can name who the vice-president is. Granted some of these tests of knowledge are dated and might have changed, but nonetheless they do speak to general civics ignorance among citizens. This is a concern for a couple of reasons. First, democratic theory and practice rests upon public opinion and it requires an informed citizenry. To be able to engage in self-rule knowledge is required. This is part of the idea of Jeffersonian democracy, expressing a faith in educated people capable of making informed decisions. Second, DelliCarpini and Keeter describe the consequences of political ignorance.

> Much of the public lacks adequate information about basic democratic norms and may, as a consequence be less committed to those norms. Poorer informed citizens hold fewer, less stable, and less consistent norms. They are more susceptible to political propaganda and less receptive to relevant new information. They are less likely to connect objective group conditions to their policy views or to connect their policy views to evaluations of public officials and political parties in instrumentally rational ways. Poorly informed citizens are less likely to participate, and when they do participate, they are less likely to tie their actions effectively to the issue stands and political orientations they profess to hold (264–265).

DelliCarpini and Keeter's documentation of the knowledge gap among citizens is reinforced in other political science literature noting correlations between education and civic engagement—those better educated and informed about the American political process generally participate more and are more supportive of basic democratic norms regarding individual rights and liberties (Miller and Shanks 1996). Conversely, their concern, about those who are politically ignorant are more susceptible of manipulation, echoes many of the American founding fathers who worried about direct democracy or rule by the people because of the public's factional, passionate, and almost impetuous nature. John Jay, the first

DOI: 10.1057/9781137308733

Supreme Court Chief Justice, as well as one of the constitutional framers and authors of the Federalist Papers, reputedly remarked that "[W]hen the pot boils, the scum always rises to the top." His reference here was to his disdain for the rule by ordinary people. In another context he simply stated: "The people who own the country should rule it."

Further proof of the ignorance or a conscious choice not to pay attention to facts surrounds Barack Obama. In 2009 23% of the population did not believe Obama was a U.S. citizen. In 2011, still a quarter of the population held this view with 40% thinking there is "cause to wonder" about his citizenship (Blanton 2011). Thus the "birther" controversy persists. Similarly, the Pew Research Center reported in 2010 that 18% of Americans think the president is Muslim, up from 11% in 2009.

But in addition to simply documenting the apparent growing ignorance of American citizens, one can turn to news consumption as a sign of changing civic literacy. Where do people go for news? In February 2000, the Pew Research Center for the People and the Press released a report entitled "The Tough Job of Communicating with the Voter." In this February 5, 2000 study, Pew noted a decline in traditional media viewing for news and rise of talk shows as a new source of news, based upon polling data it had obtained. In its survey, Pew noted that 24% rely on national TV news for political information, 25% rely on local news for campaign coverage, 31% rely on newspapers, and only 15% relied on news magazines such as *Time* or *Newsweek* as their primary source for news and information. The study also found that political activists received much of their political information from newspapers, but that marginal voters (those who do not consistently vote from election to election) received much of theirs from news magazines. More surprisingly, 51% of those surveyed indicated that they gleaned information from comedy programs such as Saturday Night Live, and 9% said they regularly received political information from Letterman or Leno.

For those under age 30, 47% indicted that they were regularly informed by late-night comedy shows. Clearly, late-night television, especially for younger and less-involved or less-informed voters, had become a staple of political information and knowledge. In fact, Goldthwaite (2002) finds evidence that there is some priming affect from late-night television among those who have less political knowledge. That means that late-night television provides cues for the politically uninformed, offering them some knowledge about candidates, which they eventually use when making up their minds about voting.

DOI: 10.1057/9781137308733

Fernando (2003) also examined the impact of late-night television on viewers of less than 30 years of age. He found that Letterman's largest demographic was the 18 to 30 age group (80), and they were most likely to gets news from late-night television (81). While Fernando did not find that political participation was affected by viewing late-night television (89, 91), he did find that it affects the images of candidates (87), especially among those who have less formal education and are less politically active (ages 18 to 24). Put into perspective, Gerald Pomper (2001) indicated that 18- to 29-year-olds represented approximately 17% of the voters in the 2000 presidential race. This means that 18,840,000 individuals in this age group voted (139). However it is not certain what percentage of this demographic considers themselves politically active or informed. But if the Pew study is accurate, around 9 million of these individuals received political information from Letterman, Leno, and the other talk shows.

In fact, alternative venues are the sources where many people now secure their political news. The Daily Show draws more 18- to 34-year-olds as viewers than any other news source. A 2007 Pew Research Center found that 16% of Americans regularly watch Comedy Central for news. But despite this, the average age of viewers of The Daily Show has risen to 41.4 (Teten 2011–12). Overall, for many segments of the population, gathering information from traditional news sources has declined. This does not necessarily mean citizens are not well informed since the new and social media may provide significant and potentially relevant political information. However, there is a real concern that these news sources are not providing adequate information to many individuals who increasingly and exclusively rely on them for knowledge about the world.

But in addition to citizens not being well informed, the same may be true of elected officials and perhaps other policy makers. Paul Gary Wyckoff's *Policy and Evidence in a Partisan Age* (2009) highlights the lack of understanding in economics among members in Congress, finding few with any formal training and literacy in this field. He also points out that often what elected officials use as evidence for their ideas are antidotal stories—the least reliable types of evidence there is. Few seem to grasp statistics, regression, or correlations and what they mean.

So what does all this mean? It suggests policy makers are often unable to grasp or understand social science evidence when making laws or designing programs. It also reveals a public ignorant about many

DOI: 10.1057/9781137308733

facets of government and politics and therefore unable perhaps to move beyond myth when making policy and candidate judgments. Should we worry about this? Should policy making be informed by facts or is all this simply about expressing values and hopes about taxes, immigration, convention centers, and a host of other issues? Even among academics there is a debate over the connection between facts and policy.

On the one hand Woodrow Wilson (1887) articulates the classic politics–administration dichotomy, seeing in the former a realm of normative values and the latter a world of scientific rationality. There is a hint here that the two should not be joined, at least in the sense that politics is about value production and thus not readily informed by the kind of research done by administrators. There are some who argue more explicitly that policy making should not be guided by social science evidence. Daniel Patrick Moynihan's *Maximum Feasible Misunderstanding* is the clearest statement on this point where he asserts: "The role of social science lies not in the formulation of social policy, but in the measurement of its results" (1969: 193). Moynihan's argument that the policy process should not be driven by social science research is indebted to the fact/value distinction articulated by David Hume (1980). The making of policy is normative; it is about making value choices about specific issues of concern. These include, for example, decisions about whether taxes are too high or too low, whether employment should increase or not. These are not factual questions that lend themselves to data or empirical resolution for scholars such as Moynihan. Instead they are preferences or goals that are less the product of evidentiary choice than they reflect political decisions. Conversely, social science evidence is entirely appropriate to use for the purposes of policy evaluation, providing important data for assessment and testing of policies to improve their efficiency or efficacy.

Moynihan's strict separation of policy making from social science evidence is not shared by all. Others reject this divorce, arguing instead that policy making should be social science-driven if the government is to improve its performance and outcomes. Alice Rivlin's *Systematic Thinking for Social Action* is the classic book on this point, lamenting the ignorance about service delivery and arguing that we ought to use federalism and random innovation to ascertain what policies work (86–90). Other works such as Edward Tufte's *Data Analysis for Politics and Policy* (1974), Martin Rein's *Social Science and Public Policy* (1976), and Charles Lindblom and David Cohen's *Usable Knowledge: Social Science and Social Problem Solving*

DOI: 10.1057/9781137308733

(1979) reach similar conclusions. For Rein (1976: 254–260) there is an inextricable connection between how values structure facts and how the latter help us to understand the former. Lindblom and Cohen (1979: 16) see professional social inquiry as providing knowledge for social problem solving.

Finally, Tufte (1974) demonstrates how empirical knowledge can facilitate policy choices. He rejects a more wooden model that distinguishes facts from values. Such a perspective also undervalues the important role that social science and other evidence can have not just in terms of helping to evaluate policies, but also in their implementation. In fact, classic models of the policy process, such as those offered by Charles O. Jones (1977) suggest a feedback loop from policy evaluation and analysis back to the beginning of the formulation stage. What this means is that once policy is made and implemented, it is then evaluated and the results of the evaluation should provide valuable data to policy makers in terms of what works or does not, providing guidance for correcting or improving the law or policy. Thus, the existence of a feedback loop reveals a preference among the policy making scholars and experts for facts to help guide the crafting of laws. We learn by doing and can improve how things work but learning from experience. Another way to state this is simply to assert that laws and legislating should not be done in a vacuum. Congress and other legislative bodies have fact-finding authority and the presumption is that the purpose of gathering information is to facilitate making better policy. Gather facts so that the laws that are written reflect what is actually known and not what is hoped for.

So think about it. The policy literature and evaluation process suggests that social science evidence and facts ought to inform the policy making process. Public pressure increasingly demands or encourages that policies be made in light of what works. Congressional and legislative fact-finding authority suggests that these bodies are expected to be informed when making laws, and common sense simply suggests that one should have facts at hand before making choices. Those who work in business or have attended MBA programs also are taught that we need to learn from our mistakes and failures if we want to improve. But this does not appear to be the case when it comes to the making of public policy in many cases.

This book discusses American politics in the age of ignorance. The assumption, thesis, and focus are simple. The assumption is that the making of policy should be informed by the best available evidence at

DOI: 10.1057/9781137308733

hand. The thesis is that more often than not policy is not made or formulated in light of what we know actually works or not. Instead, oftentimes policy is made despite the fact that good evidence suggests that a specific course or action or idea will fail, or has repeatedly failed in the past, or that there is paltry evidence that it will be successful. The focus of the book will be to identify, at the state level, several policy ideas that are repeatedly enacted when there is good evidence that they will fail. This book is not composed of original research arguing or presenting evidence about the failure of specific policies. Instead, it reviews the evidence and research that already exists surrounding a cluster of policies and ideas that are often repeated and reenacted across many states. The aim of the book is to demonstrate that evidence exists already that many of the policies often touted by public officials are will probably fail. This is the primary task of the book—simply to provide a catalog or list of policies that are often repeated or discussed with no apparent indication that the debate is informed or enhanced by research or evidence. Finally, the book will offer some ideas to explain why policy is made under these conditions of ignorance.

For the purpose of this book, ignorance means what? It refers to the fact that often times specific ideas such as the building of sports stadiums for economic development, or tax cuts to encourage business relocations, have been repeatedly employed or tried in the past, with little evidence of their success being demonstrated. Ignorance refers also to adoption of proposals or legislative ideas despite the fact that the best evidence available suggests that they will not be successful in securing their stated aim. Of course there are times when policy experiments are necessary to gain new knowledge, but researchers know that experiments are designed in light of what is already known. The same should be true with social and economic policy. But this is part of what ignorance references—not even considering the evidence when perhaps experimenting in the development of new policies.

What is not argued here is that scientists and social scientists know what the right answers are. Instead, as the book will make clear, research by social or natural scientists often can serve to eliminate bad ideas or refine existing ones. Moreover, there is no claim that there are philosopher kings or omniscient technocrats out there that know the correct answers and that they are the most fit to rule. Even among good-faith researchers seeking to find correct answers there are often debates about what is known regarding a specific issue and it is often hard to sort out

DOI: 10.1057/9781137308733

truth. But now throw in think tanks and groups spinning truth, with the media often incapable or digesting this material, and legislators and policy makers unable to make sense of it, and it is no surprise that ignorance prevails.

One objection to all of these arguments is that in a representative democracy such as the United States the majority gets the right to have its say—including being wrong. Majority rule is generally a powerful and fair way to resolve debates and issues but the ideal should be where the final decision is the product of facts and reasoned debate. There is no requirement that governing should be based on facts and not hope or belief, but it would be better if it did.

This book speaks to a gap between social science research and the legislative process. As one who has worked in government, now teaching and doing research, and who has been called upon as an expert witness to testify both in court and at the state and local legislative levels (in addition to advising members of the executive branch in formulating policy), these experiences speak to how academics and policy makers often fail to communicate and often talk past one another. Academic and applied research often suggests certain things will or will not work or that specific policy approaches have merit or not, but often this information is ignored by individuals who make policy. As someone who believes that policy ought to be evidence or fact-based, this is frustrating. The hope in writing this book is to unmask some of the ill- or badly informed ideas that dominate policy-making and to offer ideas regarding how to make a law making process that is better informed and functional.

DOI: 10.1057/9781137308733

1

States as Laboratories of Futility

Abstract: *Contemporary American political debate often criticizes the national government as an inflexible and inefficient policy maker and deliverer. Instead, some emphasize the virtues of federalism. States are depicted as laboratories of innovation, able to respond quickly to the local demands of their people and fashion creative solutions to pressing political and policy problems. But the reality is that states are often less engines of innovation than replication, reproducing ideas or programs that have been fashioned or formulated elsewhere. While in some cases this replication is good, but in many others states simply adopted failed policies found elsewhere or legislate ideas premised upon political myths, generally without any evidence of their efficacy.*

Keywords: laboratories of democracy, federalism, failed public policies, innovation, policy making process, political myths

Schultz, David. *American Politics in the Age of Ignorance: Why Lawmakers Choose Belief over Research.* New York: Palgrave Macmillan, 2013. DOI: 10.1057/9781137308733.

> Those who cannot remember the past are condemned to repeat it.
>
> George Santayana

President Barack Obama spent $700 billion in 2009 to stimulate the American economy. How that money was spent and what impact it had raises a host of interesting questions about how to achieve the proverbial "biggest bang for the biggest buck." In contemplating this stimulus plan for the economy significant talk centered on perhaps giving this money to states for them to spend on "shovel ready" projects that could potentially generate up to 4 million jobs. But the spending of this money and giving authority to the states to decide which projects to spend on raises three questions. First, how good are states in spending money to encourage economic development or engaging in good policy making? Second, are some types of project better than others to help the economy? Finally, stepping back from economic development one can ask, in general, how good are states in terms of making policy informed by data and evidence.

States are often viewed favorably as innovators in making law. Or, in the language of government officials, they are innovators in public policy. Justice Louis Brandeis' famous and often repeated quote in *New State Ice Company v. Liebman*, 285 U.S. 262 (1932) described states as laboratories of democracy where "a single courageous state may, if its citizens choose, serve as a laboratory; and try novel social and economic experiments without risk to the rest of the country." Similarly, Carl E. Van Horn, in lauding the perceived [re]newed capacity of states to innovate and experiment in public policy, asserts that "Today, at the beginning of the twenty-first century, state governments are at the cutting edge of political and public policy reform" (2006: 1). During the 2012 presidential campaign heaps of scorn and criticism were thrown upon the federal government. Republicans criticized measures such as the Patient Protection and Affordability Care Act ("Obamacare" or the Obama Health Care Act) as stealing power away from the states. Debates in Arizona and Georgia regarding state authority to regulate immigration landed in the Supreme Court (as did the individual mandate for the Obama Health Care Act) raising constitutional questions over the scope of federal versus state power. Other issues, such as same-sex marriage, also raise concerns about federalism and assertions that the federal government is getting too powerful and intervening into matters where states ought to take the lead. In an era when devolution and federalism are the buzzwords among some policy makers, and at a time when others

DOI: 10.1057/9781137308733

view lawmakers in Washington as hopelessly deadlocked in partisan battles, it is no surprise that the attention has shifted back to states to drive the policy process.

Yet while states, by default or design, may be forced to drive policy making, questions about their capacity to innovate and implement are still open to debate. It was not too long ago—perhaps only a generation or two ago—that states were viewed as hotbeds of parochialism and racism. It was as early as James Madison, who in Federalist Number 10 worried about factions dominating small republics and communities.

> The influence of factious leaders may kindle a flame within their particular States, but will be unable to spread a general conflagration through the other States. A religious sect may degenerate into a political faction in a part of the Confederacy; but the variety of sects dispersed over the entire face of it must secure the national councils against any danger from that source. A rage for paper money, for an abolition of debts, for an equal division of property, or for any other improper or wicked project, will be less apt to pervade the whole body of the Union than a particular member of it; in the same proportion as such a malady is more likely to taint a particular county or district, than an entire State (Hamilton et al. 1937: 61–62).

States were depicted as cauldrons of passion and faction. Left unchecked, state and local governments could threaten individual liberty. Madison's solution, again as proposed in Federalist Number 10, was to create a federal republic with a larger diversity of groups and interests.

> The smaller the society, the fewer probably will be the distinct parties and interests composing it; the fewer the distinct parties and interests, the more frequently will a majority be found of the same party; and the smaller the number of individuals composing a majority, and the smaller the compass within which they are placed, the more easily will they concert and execute their plans of oppression. Extend the sphere, and you take in a greater variety of parties and interests; you make it less probable that a majority of the whole will have a common motive to invade the rights of other citizens; or if such a common motive exists, it will be more difficult for all who feel it to discover their own strength, and to act in unison with each other. Besides other impediments, it may be remarked that, where there is a consciousness of unjust or dishonorable purposes, communication is always checked by distrust in proportion to the number whose concurrence is necessary (Hamilton et al.: 60–61).

Federalism and the creation of national government was made necessary to protect individual freedom, but also to bring unity to the United States

DOI: 10.1057/9781137308733

and prevent individual states from competing and discriminating against one another. The goal was to create a United States not a disunited one as the Articles of Confederation government was. Moreover, as American history would soon reveal, states were often inefficient and incompetent backwater governments that often discriminated against minorities. States, and the cities that composed them, were models of corruption, with their own Tammany Halls and political machines. Lincoln Steffens' early-twentieth-century *Shame of the Cities* is a classic tale of local corruption (2011).

But some now assert that states have moved beyond those days. As a result of Supreme Court decisions that mandate legislative redistricting, the political process is more open now. Anti-discrimination laws, better professionalism, and a host of other reforms have similarly improved the capacity of states to make policy, thereby justifying the call to return more power to the states.

Yet even though Daniel Elazar (1984) has asserted that states have different political and legal cultures that affect how their institutions are set up and operate, and Putnam (2000) has argued that the levels of social capital across the country demonstrate contrasting capacity performance, one can question whether states truly are the laboratories of democracy that Brandeis described.

When states make policy, the reality may demonstrate more often than not that they are less laboratories of democracy and more factories of replication. For example, many state legislatures are not professional or full time, or they lack extensive research staff to undertake policy work (Rosenthal 1998). The reality is that often the practice one state adopts (or state legislators take when seeking to make policy) is to ask whether another has already enacted it. As an expert witness appearing before legislative committees, inquiring into whether another state had already enacted a similar policy was one of the first questions asked. If another state did legislate on the subject at hand, often that policy was adopted, subject to minor modifications. Additionally, states may find out about legislation at conferences, such as the National Council of State Legislatures, where they hear about or see programs that have been adopted elsewhere. Or some states have become national policy leaders, such as California or New York, or others become regional leaders to which other local states look to for guidance. In many cases this guidance is good, but as Peter Schrag (2004) points out in *Paradise Lost: California's Experience, America's Future*, ideas or experiments in one

DOI: 10.1057/9781137308733

state—here California's experiment with governance by initiative and referendum—demonstrates the problems such a model may have for the rest of the country.

The point here is that states may be creatures of "me tooism," repeating and replicating policy initiatives found in other states, often adopting them without asking whether in fact they work. One of the darker or unfortunate sides to this policy diffusion and replication is that ideas adopted in one state that do not work might also be adopted elsewhere, only to reproduce policy failures across borders.

There is a need to examine the process of how state and local governments borrowing ideas from one another, often legislating from the position of ignorance. American public policy is cloaked in many myths. Encompassing such issues as public subsidies for sports stadia, tax breaks and enterprise zones, and welfare migration, there are many ideas recycled from government to government with little thought given to the evidence supporting their empirical assumptions or their prospects for success. Like bad meals that repeat on a diner, or a vampire who never dies, these ideas too are recycled and never seem to go away. This book examines several of the leading ideas and myths dominating American policy making, exploring the reasons for their repetition and the evidence for their failures. The real question raised here is simple: Why do governments consistently enact policies and laws that have already been shown to be failures?

The patterns of policy process

"Innovation [is] an idea perceived as new by an individual" (Gray 1973: 1174). Yet however much Brandeis' laboratories-of-democracy image is invoked, seldom have policy innovation and genesis been studied, at least from the point of view of examining the role that imitation takes on. Instead, a host of related issues are generally explored. Additionally, the genesis and perpetuation of bad policy ideas is not an object of inquiry in policy studies.

One set of literature explores the agenda setting process and how ideas surface, and foment. John Kingdon's *Agendas, Alternatives, and Public Policies* (1995) explains why specific policy ideas make it on to the agenda. He argues that one needs to look to policy windows and entrepreneurs where three streams—problem, policy, and politics—converge.

DOI: 10.1057/9781137308733

Specifically, while many worthy ideas might merit consideration and compete for space on the limited platform for Congress or legislatures to consider, successful policy makers or entrepreneurs benefit from the luck of a specific issue being perceived as a problem, a particular policy being seen as an appropriate to it, and political timing making consideration of the problem and policy salient.

Cobb and Elder (1972), like Kingdon, seek to understand why some ideas are thrust on to the policy agenda. They argue that triggering devices are critical to that occurring. For example, external events, such as wars or new international conflicts can place items on the agenda. The events of 9/11 placed terrorism on the national and local policy agendas, as did the launching of Sputnik back in 1957 place science and math on the education agenda. Triggering devices can also be internal events. For example, the rise of AIDS as a health threat in the 1980s, or domestic abuse in the 1970s as highlighted by the women's movements of that decade, both fit the bill as events changing the policy agenda.

Anthony Downs (1972) looks at agenda setting and issue identification in yet another way, seeing a pattern to how most policies are addressed. His issue attention cycle starts with a pre-problem stage where phenomena are not defined or seen as a problem. At some point an event, perhaps a triggering device, as described by Cobb and Elder, leads to an alarmed discovery and euphoric enthusiasm that a problem exists and that the government can in fact do something about it. However, in stage three the public and policy lawmakers come to realize the cost of significant progress, or see that addressing a problem—such as eradicating poverty—will not be quick, easy, and cheap. As a result, there is a gradual decline in public interest in addressing the problem, and finally the cycle moves into the post-problem stage where almost like the hero in an old western, the policy and issues surrounding it fade off in the sunset. Downs' model, describing policies almost in Warholian 15 minutes of fame logic, makes the five stages of the policy issue attention cycle feel like Elisabeth Kübler-Ross' (1973) five stages of dying—denial, anger, bargaining, depression, and acceptance. Other writers, such as Jones (1977) and Pressman and Wildavsky (1973) also examine agenda setting and the difficulty of getting ideas into legislative consideration.

Finally, while the policy literature often tries to explained why items make it on to the agenda, Bachrach and Baratz (1962) became interested in explaining why some items are kept off it. Their "Two Faces of Power" was a groundbreaking essay describing non-decision making. For

DOI: 10.1057/9781137308733

Bachrach and Baratz, the ability to put or not put issues on the agenda is a powerful way to influence debate. Moreover, non-decision making is still a form of policy making, especially if done repeatedly and consistently over time, when done as a result of decisions by powerful interests or elites. For example, the general lack of regulation of tobacco products, firearms, or significant reform in health care delivery in the United States may perhaps be seen as the result of non-decision making at the behest of the cigarette industry, the National Rifle Association, and the private insurance lobby as well as the American Medical Association, respectively. In just the past few years, shootings at Virginia Tech and Aurora, Colorado, as well as the one involving former Congresswoman Gabriel Giffords, should have led to renewed debate about gun control in the United States. But it may be a testament to the power of the gun lobby that such an issue stays off the policy agenda.

In parallel fashion Schattschneider's (1960) concept of the mobilization of bias in American politics is also supposed to explain why certain issues of interest to one social economic stratum are given consideration in American politics, whereas others are not. In fact, the entire pluralist school and its critiques offer suggestions on how the bargaining process among interest groups explains what issues appear or disappear from the policy frontier (Truman 1971; Schattschneider 1960; Lowi 1969: Key 1967: McConnell 1966; Dahl 1971; Dahl 1976: Dahl 1979; Dahl 1989; Baumgartner et al. 1998; Ziegler 1964). Finally, as noted in the introduction, when it actually comes to evaluation and impact, there is a rich literature in the policy analysis field demonstrating how empirical knowledge can facilitate policy choices.

What this latter group of writers seems to be hinting at is perhaps most closely related to one issue or theme of this book—the role of evidence in the policy process. First, these authors split over whether and how social science research should impact the policy making process. Second, they seem to hint at a gulf in the policy field. By that, there are many policies that have been heavily and repeatedly researched by social scientists and a significant amount of data are available either to indicate what works or not, or at least to help frame the debate about certain issues. Yet in many cases, despite the social science research, elected officials and policy makers tend to make choices as if in denial about the facts or about what the research suggests.

Overall, while policy making, especially at the state level, shows a capacity to change and innovate, the nature of that innovation is often

DOI: 10.1057/9781137308733

understudied. Ignored is how much states act as copycats to replicate what has been done elsewhere, and also overlooked is how this type of policy making is often done unreflectively, adopting proposals that have been tried elsewhere and failed. Perhaps this is done either with ignorance of this fact or with the eternal hope of a Chicago Cubs baseball fan that this time or next year it will be different.

Failed policies and political myths

Failed public policies and political myths often appear to capture the imagination of political elites. By "failed public policies" is it meant policies that are repeatedly proposed and which continuously fail, even though there is social science research indicating that these policies would not work, or at least secure the stated aims of the policy. In addition, "political myths" refer to ideas which, like the proverbial urban folk legends that seem to circulate everywhere, are often repeated or held up as true, even though there is no hard evidence to support them or worse, data contradicting them. It is bad enough that one state or policy making unit would fall prey to these policies or myths, but if states are less the laboratories of democracy and more the factories of invention than thought, then these ideas may well replicate themselves over and over, never to die the deaths they deserve.

What the remainder of the book examines are failed policies and myths. It is not an examination of government experiment to find answers. This should be lauded and often the only way to learn is to experiment. Nor is the book focused on situations were public officials simply make mistakes; yes, public officials can gather facts, do their home work, and make policy decisions that go wrong or fail for countless reasons. Instead, this is a book about policy making taking place in an environment of ignorance, where perhaps little effort is made to become informed, or facts and evidence exist but are negligently or willfully ignored. Public officials often may need to be bold and lead; this is not an indictment of that. Instead it is an indictment against acting contrary to the available evidence at hand, opting to act upon myths or ideas that simply are incorrect.

Unfortunately there are too many failed public policies and political myths to count, necessitating an eventual book to catalog them. The remainder of this book seeks to review a handful of failed policies and

DOI: 10.1057/9781137308733

myths that seem most prevalent and often repeated. It is an effort to provide guidance to a new president, Congress, and states as they think about how to spend their money for a variety of public policy purposes. It is also a guide to citizens and voters to become educated about these ideas so that the next time they hear a politician trot out one of these ideas they will be better informed about whether the idea can work or not.

The failed policies and myths which are the subject of this book are:

Tax incentives are a good way to affect business relocation decisions.
High taxes serve as deterrent to work or business activity.
Enterprise zones are an efficient means to encourage economic development.
Public subsidies for sports stadia are a good economic development tool. The building of convention and other entertainment centers are successful tools for economic development.
Welfare recipients migrate from state to state simply to seek higher benefits.
Three strikes laws and mandatory minimums are effective deterrents to crime.
Sex education causes teenagers to engage in sexual activity.
Immigration and immigrants take jobs away from Americans and serve as a drain on the economy.
Voter photo identification is needed to address widespread election fraud in the United States.
Legislative term limits will dismantle incumbent advantages, break ties to special interests, and discourage career politicians.

These failed policies and political myths fall into clusters for the purposes of how they will be treated here. The first three deal with taxes and tax incentives as tools or detriments to business activity. The second two topics look at urban development projects as tools of economic development. The next four cover a variety of social issues and the last two look at political or election myths. These are not the only failed policies and political myths that exist; they simply seem to be the ones most often repeated or debated and enacted. Because of their saliency and often reenactment, the policies are the ones that most deserve to be revealed as failed and based on myths.

DOI: 10.1057/9781137308733

2
The Truth about Taxes—
They Don't Matter Much

Abstract: *Americans have hated taxes ever since the dumping of tea into the Boston Harbor in 1773. Yet despite this hatred, many believe that taxes are a major determinant affecting economic behavior. They contend high taxes are a detriment to economic growth and that tax cuts will help induce economic growth and relocation of businesses. The reality is that in many cases, taxes have marginal impact upon economic behavior, and they generally rank low in terms of factors that affect business investment behavior.*

Keywords: Taxes, enterprise zones, business relocation, state taxes, economic development

Schultz, David. *American Politics in the Age of Ignorance: Why Lawmakers Choose Belief over Research.* New York: Palgrave Macmillan, 2013. DOI: 10.1057/9781137308733.

DOI: 10.1057/9781137308733

Americans hate taxes. It started with the dumping of tea into the Boston Harbor in 1773 to protest British treatment of the American colonies and it has never ended. The story of the United States perhaps could be told from the history of how much we dislike taxes. Henry David Thoreau went to jail because he refused to pay taxes he contended were supporting slavery. Howard Jarvis led California on a tax revolt in 1978 when voters in that state approved Proposition13, freezing property taxes on most residential property. Ronald Reagan was elected president in 1980 on the promise to cut taxes as a means of bolstering the economy. Members of the Tea Party contend that taxes are too high and must be cut to shrink the size of the federal government. And Republican presidential candidates in 2011–12—along with a host of other candidates from other offices across party labels—demand that taxes be cut or that the Bush era tax cuts become permanent in order to encourage economic growth.

Talk of taxes in the United States and one gets two opposing opinions. One is that taxes, in the words of Teddy Roosevelt, are the "price of civilization." The contrary view is one of dread—death and taxes are linked as two inevitabilities—neither of which is viewed favorably. But beyond the simple dislike or begrudging tolerance of taxes, there is also a firm belief held by many that taxes are almost magical. Significantly increase taxes and it will deter economic activity, whether it be personal or at the business level. Conversely, lower taxes create incentives to invest and grow the economy. There is a belief that taxes, properly structured, can have a significant impact upon a wide range of economic activities. As the logic goes, individuals and businesses are rational calculators—the *homo economicus* or economic man according to the world of economic theory—and decisions to act, such as to invest, save, or move, are based solely, if not exclusively, upon whether a specific option makes economic sense. If the cost of doing X is less than the benefits, then it is worthwhile to act. Create the appropriate level of taxes and one can induce the desired economic behavior. The taxman, as the Beatles song waxed, can affect economic prosperity.

The 2012 elections are typical of others in that taxes and the economy are central issues. But in reality, what do we know about taxes as they affect economic behavior?

The hype on taxes: they don't matter much

"Taxes impede economic growth." This is the belief held firmly among the Republican presidential contenders as they outmuscled one another

DOI: 10.1057/9781137308733

in 2011 and 2012 as the one who could offer the boldest plan to cut taxes as a panacea to stimulate the economy. Herman Cain wanted a tax holiday for monies held by American corporations in foreign accounts. His "9–9–9" plan assumed lower income tax rates for corporations and individuals would stimulate the economy. Newt Gingrich wanted to cap top individual income rates at 15% and Rick Perry had called for a national flat tax of 20%. Mitt Romney has a 59-point plan that includes tax cuts. Ron Paul wanted a constitutional amendment to eliminate income and estate taxes. All of the candidates promised to make the Bush-era tax cuts permanent. Michelle Bachmann wanted a return to the Reagan-era tax cuts, even though it was not clear what that really meant.

Yet do high taxes really hurt the economy as much as they believe and will lowering them have much of an impact on stimulating it? Anecdotal stories and illustrations question this tax fallacy. For example, high tax states such as Minnesota have generally fared better in terms of economic growth, unemployment, median family incomes, and location of Fortune 500 companies than low tax ones such as Mississippi and Alabama. If taxes were the only factor affecting economic growth, for example, then Mississippi would be thriving, Minnesota in the tanks. At best, there is little correlation between taxes, income, and unemployment rates, but in many situations high taxes, and with that, government expenditures on education, workforce training, and infrastructure, correlate positively with income and low unemployment and business retention. One needs to look not just at one side of the equation—taxes—but the other side too—what taxes buy—to see what value businesses get out of them in terms of educated workforces and infrastructure investments. Most debates fail to do this.

As an initial approach to exploring the relationship between taxes and economic growth one can look at data from the Bureau of Economic Analysis. Here one can compare annual economic growth as measured by the percentage change in the gross domestic product (GDP) based on current dollars, comparing it to the highest federal individual marginal tax rate and the top corporate tax rate since 1930. Effectively, this is looking at the relationship between economic growth and the tax rates on the wealthy and corporations. If taxes are a factor affecting economic growth, one should see an inverse relationship between growth of the U.S. economy and higher tax rates. Thus, for advocates of supply side economics, decreases in top marginal tax rates on the wealthy and corporations should correlate with greater economic growth. The GDP

DOI: 10.1057/9781137308733

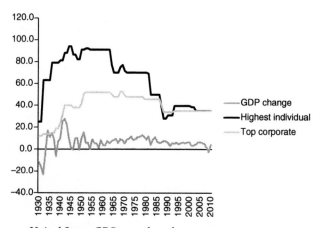

FIGURE 2.1   *United States GDP growth and taxes, 1930–2010*

should grow more quickly when top individual and corporate tax rates are lower. If taxes are a major factor deterring economic growth, lines on a graph should go in opposite directions: As tax rates go up the GDP should go down.

No such pattern emerges between high taxes and GDP growth over 80 years. During the Depression era of the 1930s corporate and individual taxes rates increased but in 1934 through 1937 the GDP grew by 17%, 11%, and 14% annually. Top corporate tax rates climbed to over 50% through the 1960s, again with no discernible pattern associated with decreased economic growth. The same is true with top tax rates on the richest, which were as high as 91% into the 1960s. Conversely, since the 1980s after Kemp–Roth tax bill (a 1981 law decreasing taxes for many in the United States) and then after 2001 with the Bush era tax cuts, there is no real indication that the economy grew more rapidly than in eras with significantly higher tax rates on the wealthy and corporations. Looking at time periods when tax rates were at their highest, GDP often grew more robustly than in periods when taxes were cut. Visually, the graph simply fails to demonstrate that tax rates negatively impact economic growth.

Pictures are worth a thousand words, but statistics are priceless. Statistically, if a tax hurts economic growth, the correlation with it is −1. If they positively facilitate growth the relationship is 1, and if they have no impact it is 0. The correlation between GDP and top individual taxes

DOI: 10.1057/9781137308733

is 0.29, between GDP and top corporate taxes is 0.32, and among the three it is 0.14. Statistically, there is a slight positive impact on either top individual or corporate taxes or economic growth, but overall almost no connection between tax rates on the wealthy and corporations and economic growth in the United States.

But what about taxes as job killers? Again running similar statistical tests, there is little connection. Using Bureau of Labor Statistics data on unemployment rates since 1940, the correlation among top individual and corporate taxes and the annual unemployment rate is −0.02—essentially no connection at all.

The simple claim of the Perry, Cain, and company that high tax rates on the wealthy and corporations hurt economic growth and job production is either false or simply overstated. The evidence is simply not there to support assertions that high taxes alone hurt the economy or that cutting them will have the stimulus effect asserted. Public investments in education, infrastructure, and worker productivity rank significantly higher in terms of encouraging economic development and higher workers' wages than do tax subsidies and incentives. Adam Smith, writing in his 1776 *Wealth of Nations*, first pointed that out, and this remains true more than 230 years later.

But one can dismiss the above analysis as simpleminded and incomplete. Maybe there is a time lag between tax cuts and economic behavior. After all, economic responses to taxes are not instantaneous but might show up several weeks, months, or years later. Perhaps in the long run taxes will be a factor affecting economic behavior. Yes, perhaps, but John Maynard Keynes, a famous twentieth-century economist, is famous for saying, "In the long run we are all dead." Taxes may have an impact that must be calculated over the long term but waiting for such effects maybe like waiting for Godot. However the above data over nearly 80 years fail to show any long-term patterns. Conversely, maybe one can assert that examining the relationship between top rates and growth is the wrong benchmark for a study, or that the analysis above is incomplete. Perhaps one needs to really look at effective tax rates—what people and corporations really pay—to tease out the real impact of taxes. There could be any of a handful of objections to the above quick analysis, but they all point to what is for some obvious— that taxes can be used as tools to induce economic behavior. All this is fair criticism.

Thus the first cluster of failed policies and political myths to examine surround taxes as tools for economic development. What does social

DOI: 10.1057/9781137308733

science research tell us about taxes and economic growth, investment, and business relocation decisions?

Taxes and business location decisions

Perhaps at the top of any list of political myths is the idea that *taxes, including their incidences and incentives, are serious factors affecting business relocation decisions* (Snell 1998). At the core of this belief is the idea that businesses make decisions about where to locate a facility based primarily, or perhaps even exclusively, upon taxes. As a result of this belief, state and local governments have engaged in dramatic tax wars against one another in order to lure businesses to their community. What do we really know about the impact of taxes upon business relocation decisions?

The literature is clear—tax breaks to encourage economic relocation are economically inefficient and wasteful. Hundreds of studies, including a bevy of them cataloged in *State Tax Notes* (Wasylenko 1997), reach this conclusion (Anderson and Wassmer 2000; Bartik 1991; Fisher and Peters 1997). Michael Kieschnick (1981) reviews numerous studies and methodologies examining the role of tax incentives on business location decisions. He concludes: "Even though there were considerable variations in the specific questions asked, the types of firms in the sample, and the areas in the country, taxes and financial inducements were consistently ranked in the bottom one-fifth or one-tenth of factors mentioned by respondents" (53). According to Michael Wasylenko (1997) in his *State Tax Notes* survey of the economic literature and studies on the impact of taxes on business location decisions:

> Two recent literature reviews (Lynch 1996; Kusmin 1994) find little evidence that the level of state and local taxation figures prominently in business location decisions. Lynch, in particular, notes that there is no evidence that state and local tax cuts, when paid for by reducing public services, stimulate economic activity or create jobs. Moreover, state and local tax incentives and financial inducements are not the only or even the primary influences on business location decisions. (1889)

Still other studies reach a similar conclusion. Roger Schmenner (1982) notes how economists see taxes as having minimal impact on business location decisions, even though economic development practitioners and elected officials disregard his evidence. Bartik (1991) reviewed 84

DOI: 10.1057/9781137308733

econometric studies undertaken since 1979 examining the role of tax incentives, generally finding that that taxes were inelastic—that is, relative changes in taxes across regions had little impact on location decisions.

Kieschnick (1995) updates his earlier research and that by Bartik (1991). He performs a meta-regression analysis that examines the empirical results found in other studies. In effect, he combines the results from numerous previous studies on tax incentives, controlling for some inconsistencies in methodologies. Kieschnick concludes by stating that his results generally confirm Bartik's results (1995).

When businesses are surveyed regarding factors important to their economic [re]location, taxes often come in way behind proximity to markets, suppliers, and the quality of the labor force (Wasylenko 1997; Kieschnick 1981). Quality of life and the arts are also critical factors driving economic development (Markusen and Johnson 2006). None of this should come as a surprise. Many of these other factors occupy a larger percentage of a business' budget than do taxes, and all of them are far more critical to the long-term success of a business than are taxes. Speaking at a chamber of commerce event in the fall of 2011, I asked business leaders whether the then proposed Obama tax cuts would encourage them to hire workers. Unanimously their response was no—they were unwilling to hire until such time that consumers were willing to buy their products and services. Consumers needed to consume before they were ready to hire anyone and lower taxes on businesses were not going to change that decision.

When pressed, businesses will actually admit to this in public. For example, nearly 62% of those interviewed in a California study on hiring tax credits indicated that they had never or rarely affected their decision to hire individuals (California Budget Project 2006). In the same study, nearly half of those interviewed stated that tax incentives for relocation did not affect their decisions (California Budget Project 2006; Hissong 2003). Overall, the economic development literature states that tax incentives and levels of taxation are not major determinants of relocation, but instead might have some marginal influence when there is some tax elasticity and where the incidence is significant compared to other contiguous jurisdictions.

The argument here is not that taxes do not matter. Instead they matter but at a lower order or in more subtle ways than chambers of commerce types of arguments would suggest. First, when decisions regarding location are being made, other factors rank higher, such as labor costs or

DOI: 10.1057/9781137308733

access to markets and suppliers. This is what businesses will first consider when making more macro or first cut decisions regarding where to locate. Once these major factors are considered then taxes become a secondary or tertiary level factor to narrow down more specific locations or jurisdictions in which to settle. At this point the question is perhaps settling within a specific city or a nearby one. Wasylenko makes this point about the marginal role of taxes at a more meso or micro level when he concludes that "This review of the literature suggests that taxes have a small, statistically significant effect on interregional location behavior" (1892). Once other factors are considered, it is here then that taxes may be a factor to determine or finalize a location choice. This makes sense. Labor for example constitutes a much greater percentage of doing business than do many other expenses. This means wages and workforce quality might be more significant factors in affecting business location decisions than are other variables. Thus, when a business adds up all of the costs and factors affecting where it should do business there may be only a handful of locations that make sense of a business to relocate to. Here is the point where businesses then pit communities against one another (LeRoy 2005). It is like the classic prisoners' dilemma. If two accomplices are separately questioned by the police, the best scenario would be for both to remain silent. If that were to occur perhaps both walk free. If one talks and confesses he goes free or gets a lesser sentence and the other gets a worse sentence. If both confess they both go to jail. No community wants to be the one taking the economic high ground and not do something. Moreover, no public official wants to look passive as neighbor rolls out the tax red carpet for a business. Thus, bidding war ensues and businesses are only too happy to encourage and take advantage of it (LeRoy 2005).

But communities cannot resist the temptation to act, even if they conclude that it is wrong; instead political considerations often intrude into economic development decisions (Malizia and Feser 1999: 257–259). Consider two recent studies. The first study entitled *An Evaluation of the Keystone Opportunity Zone (KOZ) Program* was prepared for the Pennsylvania Legislative Budget and Finance Committee in 2007. The report examined the role of tax incentives for individuals and businesses in the creation of special economic regions (enterprise zones) in order to induce economic development. While much of the report criticized inadequate data and recordkeeping that complicated accountability and appropriate analysis, it also noted that many of the claims about job

DOI: 10.1057/9781137308733

creation and capital investment by the private sector were vastly over-stated. The report concluded: "On an individual project basis, numerous KOZ projects appear to be working as intended and are rated as 'success stories', although KOZ status alone is generally not the sole contributing factor in a business' decision to locate or relocate in a KOZ" (S-8). What the Pennsylvania report found was that claims about the efficacy and impact of tax cuts alone as a major factor encouraging business location decisions were exaggerated. They might have had some impact but it was more muted than its supporters contended.

A second study entitled *Money for Something: Job Creation and Job Quality Standards in State Economic Development Subsidy Programs* was prepared for the Good Jobs First organization in 2011 by Philip Mattera and three other authors. They examined 238 state economic development programs across the 50 states and the District of Columbia. The analysis looked at a range of economic incentives that included tax cuts, subsi-dies, tax incentives, loans, and several other inducements. It is arguably one of, if not, the single most comprehensive examination of state-level economic development tools to date.

The authors document $70 billion annually for economic develop-ment, with $11 billion deployed in terms of a variety of tax incentives or programs as noted above (Mattera, i). Significant variation among state programs is noted, with only four states giving B or better grades in terms of how the programs are administered in terms of documenting results or making sure that the money is spent on jobs with good pay and health care coverage. Over half of the states earned grades of C- or worse. What the authors of the study found, as was similar to that with the Pennsylvania study, were that data gathering was often poor, per-formance exaggerated, and proof of real efficacy of the incentives ques-tionable. But beyond these points, the authors describe how the types of jobs created—in terms of wages and benefits—often were poor. Thus, even if jobs or economic development occurred as a result of the incen-tive programs offered, the impact in terms of quality jobs was debatable. As the authors state in their executive summary:

> At a time when unemployment remains high and states and cities are spend-ing an estimated $70 billion a year in the name of economic development, taxpayers are right to ask if such expenditures are creating a substantial number of good jobs. An analysis of major state economic development programs finds that many subsidy programs require little if any job crea-tion. Fewer than half provide any kind of wage standard for the workers at

subsidized companies, and fewer than a fourth require any sort of health-care coverage. (Mattera: i)

The Good Jobs First argument is slightly different from the argument asserting that taxes are not a significant factor in economic development decisions. Yes this assertion is implied in their report. With 238 programs in place across the country, the collective net effect of them is to cancel one another out. But the authors shift gears to question also about what types of jobs are being produced with taxes. They find that good jobs—those with living wages and benefits—are often wanting. Even if relocation occurred as a result of the tax incentives, the type of jobs and economic development that is actually produced is not very good.

If the empirical data on relocation decisions was not enough to show the futility of using tax incentives as an economic development tool, two additional arguments bode against it. First is the concept of efficiency; second is the notion of opportunity costs. In terms of efficiency, it is first necessary to explain two concepts—Kaldor–Hicks and Pareto efficiency.

Kaldor–Hicks efficiency simply states that some economic outcome is efficient if it produces an overall net gain in outcomes such as wealth and the winners in a decision could reimburse others for their loses. What this means is that a decision must be able to maximize outcomes or economic goods to such a degree that losers are in theory compensated for their losses. This is a simple utilitarian calculus of producing the greatest good for the greatest number of people, with the caveat that losers are paid for their losses.

Pareto efficiency refers to a situation where no one can make any further economic gains without someone losing. Thus, if by doing X I am $1 million richer but if someone loses $500,000, the decision is not Pareto efficient. Efficiency refers to situations with winners and no losers. Both types of efficiency are important because classical economics assumes free markets are both Kaldor–Hicks and Pareto efficient. This has to be the assumption about tax incentives to induce business location decisions. But the truth is that is often not the case.

First, in relocations, while one community wins, another loses (especially if there is a business or plant closing and moving to another location). Subsidizing this cost transforms what might have been a net zero impact in terms of economic costs into an overall loss scenario. By that, awarding a business a tax incentive to moves either pays entities to do something they were already planning to do or it creates a loser in a situation (the community losing jobs). On top of all that, any money that perhaps should have been awarded to the losers to make the relocation Kaldor–Hicks and Pareto efficient is lost. Simply put, this is robbing Peter to pay Paul, with Peter losing and Paul either rewarded to do what he planned to do or money that should have been given to compensate the loser diverted to the relocating business. In either case, the tax inducement is inefficient.

Tax incentives also run a problem with opportunity costs. "Opportunity costs" refers to the best way to maximize the use of a scare resource. If I have $100 to invest, can I get best returns (making money) by buying stock, depositing in the bank, or going to the racetrack? Another way to think about would be that I can either spend $100 on dinner and drinks or on books. Making one economic choice foregoes another. Opportunity costs force decisions not to be examined in isolation but in comparison to other scenarios or options. The same can be done with tax subsidies.

In terms of opportunity costs, communities contemplating tax subsidies should consider whether it would be a better use of their money to give incentives to businesses or spend the money another way if the goal is economic development. Public investments in education, infrastructure, and worker productivity rank significantly higher in terms of encouraging economic development and higher workers' wages than do tax subsidies and incentives. Kieschnick makes this point in arguing that few studies on taxes look to their value in terms of paying for education, workforce development, infrastructure, and a host of other forces that might actually aid business development (1981: 12). Adam Smith declared:

> The third and last duty of the sovereign or commonwealth is that of erecting and maintaining those public institutions and those public works, which, though they may be in the highest degree advantageous to a great society, are, however, of such a nature that the profit could never repay the expense to any individual or small number of individuals, and which it therefore cannot be expected that any individual or small number of individuals should erect or maintain (Smith 1937: 452).

What Smith understood so well is that the government can serve an important role in facilitating the conditions necessary for the market and economy to operate. Proper investments in critical areas actually promote as oppose to deter economic growth, with expenditures in education perhaps the single best tool that can be deployed for this

DOI: 10.1057/9781137308733

purpose (Luttbeg 2005). Of course such investments might take time—
way beyond the next election cycle for most elected officials anxious
to show quick results or that they are doing something. Thus, from an
opportunity costs perspective, money spent on tax incentives to induce
relocation is a bad investment even if it looks like a good idea from a
short-term political time horizon.

The bottom line: Tax subsidies and incentives for economic development do little to impact business investment decisions.

Taxes, jobs, and economic growth

A variant of the "taxes are important factors affecting location decisions"
argument is the claim *that high taxes are deterrents to economic growth
and that tax cuts will generally lead to investment decisions that produce, for
example, jobs and new employment.* This is the core of the supply side economics argument offered by some economists and politicians. Another
spin is that both individuals and entities have high elasticity when it
comes to taxes such that both flee from high to low tax jurisdictions.

For all of the same reasons that taxes are not a major factor in economic
relocation decisions, the same is true in terms of the impact of taxes on
business or individual activity. While taxes may have some minor impact
alone in terms of marginal decisions to produce, the broader claim that
they impede serious economic growth is a vastly overblown claim that
lies at the heart of supply side economic theory.

Advocates of supply side economics point to the 1964 Kennedy tax cut
(The Revenue Act of 1964) that was passed by President Johnson after
JFK was assassinated as an example of where such an action did work in
terms of stimulating the economy and increasing government revenue.
However, there are several reasons to question first whether these claims
holdup. First, the economy was already growing during this time period
and government revenues would have naturally increased because of
this. There is evidence that government revenue would have been higher
had the taxes not been cut (Samuelson and Nordhaus 2005: 6). Moreover,
there is no real evidence that the tax cuts had a major impact on the
economic growth, which was already occurring when they were passed.
However, if the tax cuts did have some impact on economic growth it
was because it placed more money in the wallets of consumers as a result
of a 20% across-the-board reduction in taxes, with some minor business

DOI: 10.1057/9781137308733

reductions too. The tax reduction here translated into more consumer demand for goods and services and that helped the economy. This tax cut worked not for supply side theory reasons (giving more money to investors to invest) but because it created more demand in the economy and that helped businesses produce more. These tax cuts also were not offset by government spending cuts. Too often now tax cuts are coupled with government reductions in spending, as were the Reagan tax cuts (Kemp–Roth) in 1981, yielding high interest rates and a significant slow-down in the economy.

In 2001 President Bush pushed through significant tax cuts on the claim that country had ample money and the federal government was running surpluses. Cutting taxes was seen again as a way to stimulate the economy. The evidence at best is inconclusive that the tax cuts had any real impact on job production or stimulating consumer behavior (Bartlett 2010; Gold 2012). Too much of the tax reduction here and with Reagan in 1981 went to those at high income levels and there is little support that these individuals significantly increased their consumption or that they invested the saved income in any type of economic develop-ment that produced jobs. Similarly, President Obama has on occasion called for special tax cuts to encourage economic development, but again either the cuts are too small, not precise to induce desired behavior, or their impact is overstated.

The point here is as with business location decisions, taxes are a rela-tively minor factor in the costs of production, falling far behind labor, transportation, supplies, and perhaps energy in terms of issues impact-ing production. Moreover, as noted above, often overlooked in studies of taxes is the net overall impact of taxes minus services that individuals and entities receive in a jurisdiction. One needs to undertake a complete calculation of what benefits are received from a jurisdiction minus the costs in taxes. It is this overall package that perhaps more appropriately should be considered when deciding what impact government taxes and spending has upon decisions to produce.

There are two additional arguments that can be marshaled in a dis-cussion of taxes and productivity. First there is the often used argument that if high taxes were the only factor affecting production decisions, then states such as Minnesota, New York, Massachusetts, and California would be economically dying or poor (in terms of per capita income, state gross domestic product, and number of Fortune 500 companies, for example) whereas Mississippi and Alabama would be prosperous and wealthy states because of their respective high and low tax incidences. However, the opposite is true, suggesting other factors are also important in affecting business and work decisions.

Second, if in fact high taxes are a deterrent to work, one would expect to see that reflected in migration work patterns among commuters. Schultz (1998; 2000b) studied the impact of state income taxes upon individuals who were tax commuters. Tax commuters are individuals who cross state lines for the purposes of work. He found little evidence that the presence or absence of income taxes, high or low income taxes, or even the presence or absence of special commuter taxes served as a deterrent to individuals crossing state jurisdictions to work. While clearly these studies are not the final word on the topic, they do suggest that other variables in addition to the presence or absence of income taxes serve as an impediment to work. In fact, assuming many individuals have a certain amount of autonomy and choice to cross jurisdictions to work, they could have engaged in tax avoidance behavior (beyond cheating!) by choosing not to commute.

Third, we will return to the discussion that began this chapter. It provided a multiyear multistate analysis of top corporate and individual tax rates in the United States, seeking to determine whether they were connected in any way with GDP growth or jobs. The simple answer was no. Over the long haul there appears no correlation with tax rates and these other variables. As also noted in the beginning of the chapter, perhaps this simple analysis is too crude or it misses critical factors that might come into play that reveal a more subtle role for taxes. Overall, the argument is not denying that in some cases taxes might serve to impact work in some marginal cases or on a micro scale. But the broader or macro claim that taxes alone discourage individual and entity production is a vastly overblown assertion.

Enterprise zones

Enterprise zones in the United States were developed as an economic development tool to revitalize depressed areas that were lacking in investment or job production. More often than not these areas were urban communities which, since the Model Cities programs of the 1960s, had been the focus of redevelopment. These were communities which some scholars had seen as creating cultures of poverty or were

DOI: 10.1057/9781137308733

areas where work and jobs had disappeared (Lewis 1969; Wilson 1997). Unfortunately, Model Cities did not work, or at least was perceived not to be working or was abandoned in the Nixon administration, and instead replaced by the Community Development Block Grant Program and Urban Development Assistance Grants. But by the 1980s even these programs were not viewed favorably and during the Reagan Administration enterprise zones became a popular idea for economic development. These zones came to be seen as development tools not just for urban cores, but for any depressed community needing an influx of capital investment. This belief in their efficacy has led to the claim that *enterprise zones are an efficient means to encourage economic development.*

Much of the logic of enterprise zones relies upon the assumptions of using tax abatements as incentives for business relocations or development or to encourage employment decisions. But in the case of enterprise zones, there is an identified geographic region that is deemed to be economically disadvantaged or needing special help. Within this zone a state or local government would provide financial incentives, such as abated or reduced income, property, sales, or other types of taxes. In some cases, a region would be eligible for all of the above. These tax incentives, along with perhaps infrastructure assistance, are supposed to induce businesses to relocate into the enterprise zone, and thereby bring with it jobs and all the benefits associated with their move.

While elegant in theory, how have enterprise zones really worked? Bottom line: They are generally a cost ineffective failure in encouraging economic development and in producing meaningful employment opportunities. As summarized by Peters and Fischer:

> Enterprise zone incentive programs do not seem to provide enough benefit to firms to materially alter their investment and locational habits; as a result, they do not induce much, if any new growth. Moreover, although enterprise zones are justified by politicians and academics alike as helping economically disadvantaged areas, zones do not appear to provide much in the way of employment opportunities to zone inhabitants. Furthermore, they tend to be very costly for government (2003: 128).

Enterprise zones suffer from three defects. First, the financial benefits (tax abatements) are too little to induce relocation decisions. Second, the jobs they produce are not meaningful or are too costly given the public investments. Third, the overall programs are costly. Add to these three a fourth criticism: Enterprise zones merely move investment from one community to another at public expense, thereby creating no new

DOI: 10.1057/9781137308733

economic gains while at the same time subsidizing relocation decisions that probably would have already occurred.

The logic of enterprise zones rests upon the same premises as the overall strategy of using taxes as a driver to induce development or relocation. This means enterprise zones are subject to the same criticisms as were described earlier in the chapter when it comes to taxes as a factor affecting business investment decisions. To repeat, as Bartik (1991; 1994), Wasylenko, (1997) and others have shown, taxes are far down on the list of factors that influence economic location decisions. They are far less important than the quality of the workforce, access to supplies and markets, and a host of other factors. Thus, for taxes to be a major factor to induce relocation they would have to be of such magnitude beyond what any government offers.

Second the job production associated with enterprise zones is spotty at best. One study in California found, for example, that nearly half of the businesses involved in an enterprise zone program stated that the tax credits had little impact on their decisions to hire individuals (California Budget Brief 2006). A 2009 report from the Public Policy Institute of California found that enterprise zones had "no statistically significant effect on job creation" (Fulton 2011; Kolko and Neumark 2009). Even a 2001 HUD study on the federal Empowerment Zones and Enterprise Communities Program could not substantiate that the job growth in these areas was statistically better from the areas outside them during the hot economic binge of the 1990s. The quality and cost of the jobs produced were also of concern in the report on these zones. The Pennsylvania Legislative Budget and Finance Committee's *An Evaluation of the Keystone Opportunity Zone (KOZ) Program* (2007) reported that "KOZ Program had resulted in the creation of 63,966 new jobs and the retention of over 48,158 jobs since the program began in 1999" (S-3). The report, once it dug into the claims, found that "KOZ jobs data was substantially overstated and not supportable" (S-3).

In Minnesota in 2003 then Governor Tim Pawlenty made enactment of JOBZ—a state-sponsored enterprise zone—one of his top economic priorities. JOBZ would provide several millions of dollars in assorted tax breaks to designated communities to encourage business relocation or retention. The non-partisan Minnesota Office of the Legislative Auditor studied implementation of the program (2008). It found from 2004 to 2008 (its first three years) 300 subsidy agreements were signed, providing $45 million in tax breaks. While the report noted

DOI: 10.1057/9781137308733

some value to the subsidies in terms of economic development, it was mostly critical of the program. It noted that subsidies were given to one business to compete against another Minnesota company, often for the same customers. In other cases the subsidy was given to a business already ready to expand, or that the subsidies often went not to areas economically hard-pressed. The study found too little concern or attention was given to negotiating jobs or wage agreements. There were also problems, as with the Pennsylvania program, in gathering data or in appropriate follow up or analysis of the subsidy agreements and what companies did.

Overall several studies, such as by Boarnet et al. (1996), Greenbaum and Engberg (2000), and Bondonio and Engberg (2000) reach similar conclusions: job and economic growth were not necessarily enhanced by enterprise zones. Even beyond their use for enterprise zones, tax breaks often fail to create the conditions for companies to hire individuals. For example, Berenson (2007) reported that even with the billions of dollars in tax breaks given to drug companies, those incentives failed to yield the jobs promised.

Third, as just noted, job production in enterprise zones seldom lives up to their hype. Surveying over 75 zones, Peters and Fischer (2003) found the average public subsidy per job to be nearly $60,000 annually, with overall costs in the millions to induce one job. This is hardly economically efficient. Moreover, in terms of providing job opportunities to those living in the zones, often they lack the requisite job skills, or those living outside the enterprise area are hired, thereby again mitigating the impact of the government as a development and opportunity program.

Finally, if other factors in addition to taxes are more important in influencing relocation and hiring decisions, what is the real impact of providing the subsidy and encouraging a move? Simply this is classic "robbing Peter to pay Paul." Businesses and jobs are closed in one community and are paid to relocate to another (that would have probably already occurred anyhow) but this time at public expense or loss of tax revenue. Hence, any gains in one area are offset by losses in another, unless one can assume that cluster development in the new area is so significant that it offsets the losses in another community.

But yet another flaw in the enterprise zone concept is again related to the same problem associated with building too many of any attraction, such as aquariums—one is novel but too many floods the market and diminishes the uniqueness of them all. If there is only one aquarium

DOI: 10.1057/9781137308733

then it enjoys a comparative advantage as a tourist attraction, but if many communities have them then the unique attraction goes away. Many states have multiple enterprise zones. While the Legislative Auditor did not focus in on it, think about another problem with JOBZ and similar programs. In Minnesota JOBZ had "1,150 separate subzones on a total of about 29,300 acres in more than 350 cities and townships" (12). If the purpose of an enterprise zone is to create a special advantage associated by being within it, having so many zones or regions simply negates their efficacy. In Minnesota, how effective can the program be if 1,150 subzones and 350 local governments are using the same tool to compete against one another? Their impact is muted and instead, there comes to be an expectation among businesses that they should get a tax break wherever they locate. If one thinks enterprise zones are a good tool for development, there cannot be too many of them lest they cancel one another out. At one time in South Carolina, the entire state was declared an enterprise zone. At some point the dilution of tax advantages from these programs negate one another, thereby rendering them ineffective within the state and then across state lines.

Overall, while a nifty idea in theory, enterprise zones have been shown to be repeated failures in producing the promised benefits.

Conclusion

No doubt that much more could be said about taxes and the economy. However, the argument of this chapter is that social science research questions the efficacy and impact that taxes alone can have upon the economy, including business investment decisions. Taxes can have marginal impacts good and bad for the economy, but among the great political myths is the exaggerated claim regarding their influence on the behavior of people and organizations. Economists like to say there are no free lunches and this is definitely true when it comes to taxes as tools of economic development. Tax cuts or incentives have costs associated with them. It is important to recognize that someone pays for the tax cuts in addition to them having marginal impact alone on the economy and businesses. But despite the evidence, why do businesses demand tax breaks? The simple answer is that they can get them. Communities are all too willing to appear "business friendly" or "open to business" and they compete against one another to lure businesses to their community.

DOI: 10.1057/9781137308733

Local governments in effect become captured by business, acting as an investment arm for them (Fitzgerald and Leigh 2002). Businesses in turn are more than happy to encourage and bait this competition. But as states and communities have increased the tax ante, their public benefits become even more questionable (Bond 2011).

DOI: 10.1057/9781137308733

3
Sportsfare—Welfare for Professional Sports

Abstract: *State and local governments often view public subsidies or construction of sports facilities and convention centers as efficient and effective tools of local economic development and jobs development. Yet investments in these types of structures generally are poor means of encouraging economic development because commitments of public funds to these types of structures generally is more costly and less productive in terms of the level of economic development or job development that results when compared to other investments such as in education. Second, because these strategies are pursued by multiple governments, their effects cancel one another out.*

Keywords: Convention center, professional sports, sports stadiums, public subsidies, economic development, jobs, *Field of Dreams*

Schultz, David. *American Politics in the Age of Ignorance: Why Lawmakers Choose Belief over Research*. New York: Palgrave Macmillan, 2013. DOI: 10.1057/9781137308733.

"If you build it he will come."

Field of Dreams

The 1989 movie *Field of Dreams* is a metaphor, if not a parody, for urban politics and development. The film features Kevin Costner's character Ray Kinsella, a farmer, who walks into his Iowa cornfield one day, only to hear a voice command "If you build it he will come." Kinsella then sees a baseball diamond with players, featuring the legendary Shoeless Joe Jackson. The movie itself is a classic fantasy baseball film replete with sports trivia and adventure as Costner's character travels across America with Terrance Mann (James Earl Jones) in search of lost youth and the dreams of glory. By the end of the movie Kinsella convinces his family that they should abandon their corn and keep the ball field as a way for not only him to reconnect with his father, who had dreams of being a baseball player, but also to recapture and renew an innocence and joy once lost. This field will attract others, luring them too to find their dreams.

The power and lure of the movie resides on several fronts. One of course is simply as a terrific baseball or sports film, appealing to all of us who wanted to grow up and be centerfielder. It is thus about the American dream. But the film also speaks to the power and logic of much urban economic development and the tourism trade. The phrase "If you build it he will come" has morphed into "If you build it they will come," referring to the idea that if a community erects some type of attraction tourists or visitors will flock to see it. Building of some spectacle—such as zoo, aquarium, convention center, casino, or even a sports facility will serve as the cornerstone for economic revitalization of a community. As someone who has worked in local government, teaches present and future local government officials, and who follows urban and suburban politics, the "If you build it they will come" mantra is often invoked to defend and promote development projects—"If it worked in the movie why not here in Anytown, USA."

What makes *Field of Dreams* so ironic is that the original setting for the film—a farm in Dyersville, Iowa—eventually itself followed the prescription of the movie, retaining the field and turning it into a tourist attraction. The movie's postmodern message turned out to be a marketing gimmick for this small Iowa town, giving it fame and some tourism that it lacked before 1989. Perhaps the movie proved to be true—if you build it they will *actually* come.

DOI: 10.1057/9781137308733

This type of logic of building a novel attraction has led to various types of economic development projects. For example, Chicago was successful in 1999 with its famous "Cows on Parade" exhibit. It featured 300 fiberglass cows along Michigan Avenue artistically dressed up in a variety of ways. Many of the cows were themed or created by famous artists, and their placement along Chicago's premier street created a buzz in the city and across the country. Suddenly other communities thought if they were to replicate this public art, others too would come. St. Paul, Minnesota featured the cartoon characters from Charles Shultz's (a St. Paul native) *Peanuts*, with Charlie Brown, Snoopy, Lucy, and Linus featured across the city. Dozens of other US cities such as Rochester, New York (horses), Pensacola, Florida (pelicans), Scranton, Pennsylvania (mules), and Baltimore, Maryland (crabs) served as copycats to replicate the excitement of Chicago's cows. All these cities and others had their own fields of dreams that providing these attractions would boost tourism and their economic fortunes as out-of-towners flocked to see their public art.

Now perhaps in Chicago and in a few other communities the public art successfully wooed visitors and helped the economy, but it is not so clear that these projects were successes across the board. Two reasons stand out for this. First, Chicago is Chicago. There are many attractions in the city and Cows on Parade was only one part in a broader mix of events and sites that tourists and art seekers would find compelling. Think of the Art Institute of Chicago, for example, as a major attraction on Michigan Avenue. It is not clear how many people came to Chicago simply or solely because of the cows. It may have been one of several factors drawing visitors, including Wrigley Field, Michigan Avenue shopping, and a host of other museums in the city. It is not so clear that Peanuts characters, mules, pelicans, or crabs are singular attractions encouraging people to visit St. Paul, Scranton, Pensacola, or Baltimore. Second, the cows on parade were novel and grand. It was novel in the sense that it was the first of its kind. Yet once something is done once, twice, and then more, the concept loses its uniqueness and excitement and it becomes routine. There is a diminishing value to overextending a brand. Moreover, the grandness of 300 cows on parade, often featuring famous artists was a powerful force behind the Chicago exhibit.

But there is definitely a copycat aspect to what the others cities did. They saw something someone else did and then figured they could replicate that success in their own community. If they could build it

DOI: 10.1057/9781137308733

elsewhere and they came, we can build it here and they too will come. In the same way that state and local governments all engage in tax wars to lure businesses; the same thing happens with economic development projects. In the 1990s it was aquariums. Inspired by Chicago's Shedd Aquarium, cities across the country saw their future in fish on display. The Mall of America in the Minnesota suburb of Bloomington originally opened with an aquarium in it. Duluth, Minnesota too opened one, as did Denver in 1999, and others were also opened in Valdez, Alaska, Albuquerque, N.M., Tampa, F.L., and Camden, N.J. But by 2002 the Denver Ocean Journey had closed, and those in Camden and Tampa and in many other cities saw significant drops in attendance as the novelty wore off. "The $52 million Camden aquarium had 1.2 million visitors its opening year, 1992, but then it dropped and leveled to around 500,000. Officials fault a lack of nearby development. Aquariums are hybrids, often called 'edutainment.' Denver City Councilwoman Susan Barnes-Gelt suggested that the country might have too many" (*Baltimore Sun* 2002). Some of these aquariums had to be restructured and now exist as a shell of their former selves.

Cities were in a rush to grab a piece of the tourist industry that they thought an aquarium could purchase. But operating them is expensive, and many fish died as communities or organizations realized that they were beyond their means to operate these facilities. But among the reasons for the failure of some of these facilities, as Barnes-Gelt indicated, was aquarium glut—there were too many of them across the country to sustain them as novel attractions. The same thing seems to be occurring with casinos. Once when Las Vegas had a monopoly on gaming it did well. The state of New Jersey opened Atlantic City to gambling and over time more and more states and communities had expanded gaming. These different jurisdictions are now competing against one another for gaming dollars. This is transforming a once-profitable attraction into something that has diminishing returns over time because of the competition and lack of novelty (Cooper 2012). At some point the novelty wears off with casinos and aquariums. The population of those who want to look at fish is limited, or perhaps if you have seen one fish the you-have-seen-them-all mentality kicks in. But there is no question that the diminishing returns of aquariums did not take too long to surface.

But the lessons of Cows on Parade and aquariums seem lost on many communities. Maybe in some cases it makes sense to support projects like these. But the rush to copycat the success of others is simply too

DOI: 10.1057/9781137308733

compelling to resist, suggesting that in many cases doing what everyone else does for economic development no longer makes sense. Novelties wear off or attractions only work in a specific location because of a host of factors unique to it. Yet on top of the rush to copycat what appears to be successful elsewhere there is another logic that seems to infect local public officials—it is the curse of the Pharaohs and the lure of the Romans. By that, the ancient Egyptian Pharaohs had pyramids built for their eternal glory. Similarly, in ancient Rome there was the Coliseum, a major attraction for gladiators and other events. These edifices are a particularly potent form of the "if you build it" logic. It seems that many government officials want their own pyramid—some big massive concrete and steel monument they can point to which was built while they were mayor or governor and which will endure well past their time in office. Sure perhaps it might make sense to fix potholes, rebuild roads, or fix aging sewer lines, but more press can be had by a ribbon-cutting ceremony in front of a new building. There simply seems to be a bigger political incentive to build an edifice as opposed to fixing potholes. This is especially the case if the structure is coliseum-like. Two examples of this stand out. The first is the construction of sports facilities, especially a new professional sports stadium. The second is erecting a convention center. Both are great examples of the "if you build it" logic, and both represent what can often be described as bad policies that are economically inefficient, wasteful, and sold as panaceas for what ails a community. This chapter examines the political myths surrounding both.

Public subsidies for professional sports

One claim often asserted is that *public subsidies for sports stadia are good economic development tools.* Does it make sense for a city or community to fund the construction of a new sports stadium in order to stimulate economic development? Listening to sports reporters, team owners, and many elected officials, the answer is yes. Yet while it may be fun to root, root, root, for the old ball team, does it make good economic policy for the public to provide tax dollars to pay, pay, pay to for new stadiums?

In 1992 the Atlanta Falcons National Football League team moved into the Georgia Dome, which cost $214 million to build. The state of Georgia donated the land for the project and the Georgia World Congress Center issued state-backed bonds to finance the construction of the facility.

DOI: 10.1057/9781137308733

Twenty years later there is now talk of replacing the Dome with a new $948 million facility, of which taxpayers would shell out $300 million (*Economist*, May 19, 2012: 36–37). In Minnesota the state will pay $348 million toward a $975 million new stadium for the NFL Vikings. This money would be financed by some extension of gaming and by issuance of appropriation bonds and some taxes on sports paraphernalia. Additionally the city of Minneapolis will contribute $150 million, making the public contribution to the project nearly a half-a-billion dollars! Minnesota's public officials told the state's taxpayers that they should be consoled by the fact that the billionaire owner Zigi Wilf would have to now pay $477 million for the new facility, $50 million more than the Vikings said they were willing to pay (Bierschbach 2012). Yet between special NFL loans, grants, and other concessions, Wilf will actually only have to put up about $30 million for his new football home (Reusse 2012). Put up $30 million to get nearly $950 million, that's a terrific return on investment.

The story of the Falcons and the Vikings underscores a public pattern of financing professional sports facilities in the United States. From 1992 until the spring of 2012, taxpayers have paid an average of 73% of the cost for football stadiums (*Economist*, May 19, 2012: 36–37). Between 1990 and 2004 the public shelled out approximately $10 billion for stadia (Rappaport and Wilkerson 2001). These stadia or stadiums are often sold to the public as great economic development tools, that they will bring jobs to a community, instill pride, or make the city a major league player (Rappaport and Wilkerson 2001). The construction of these edifices is thus described as important economic development tools for the community.

But what are the facts and what do we know about the impact of sports stadia on economic development and urban revitalization? The overwhelming evidence is that the public use of tax dollars for a sports stadium is economically inefficient and a bad investment that produces no real net economic benefit to a community. In short, giving money to building stadia is simply sportsfare or welfare for sports.

In general, as one surveys local debates about stadium construction in the United States, three basic arguments are employed to support using public money to build sports stadia. First, proponents claim that building a new stadium will have a big impact on the economy, generating many new jobs and bringing new businesses to the area (Delaney and Eckstein 2004: 22). These are either initial construction jobs or those generated

DOI: 10.1057/9781137308733

with the new stadium. However study after study has demonstrated that advocates of public spending on stadia consistently exaggerate the benefits of sports to a local economy (Delaney and Eckstein 2004; Bernstein 1998; Coates and Humphreys 2000; Baade and Dye 1990; Baade 1994; Feng 2008).

A 1996 Congressional Research Service (CRS) report, "Tax-Exempt Bonds and the Economics of Professional Sports Stadiums" (Zimmerman 1996), concluded that sports stadia represent a small percentage (generally less than 1%) of a local economy. It also stated that there is little real impact or multiplier effect associated with building sports stadia (see also Delaney and Eckstein 2004). By that, if one looks at the economic impact of the dollars invested in sports stadia, the return is significantly smaller than compared to other dollars invested in something else. Moreover, the building of stadia merely transfers consumption from one area or one type of leisure activity to another, and that overall, sports and stadia contribute little to the local economy and instead represent an investment that costs the public a lot while failing to return the initial investment. Dollar for dollar, the opportunity costs of investing in sports stadia is a terrible option if the goal is economic development or job development. In short, of the nearly $3 billion in sports subsidies Zimmerman documented, he found it produced little, at the cost of over $120,000 per job. Moreover, any new jobs produced by the new stadium need to subtract jobs lost or transferred from the existing one. There is also evidence that the spending here on sports financing has a smaller multiplier effect than spending for other projects because much of the money goes to player salaries or owners' profits and not to small local businesses or residents. Finally, in terms of construction jobs touted with the building of a stadium, just as many jobs, if not more, could be produced with any public works project, such as building a school, park, or a road. Put into perspective, the American Society of Civil Engineers in 2012 gave the country's infrastructure a grade of a D, noting a need of $2.2 trillion in investments to replace decaying bridges, roads, and water systems (Wong 2012). Were we to spend tax dollars fixing broken infrastructure at least if not more jobs would be produced and greater economic gains yielded than were the money put into sports stadium subsidies. Dollar for dollar, infrastructure spending is better for the economy than sports subsidies. However, as noted, not too many mayors find it very sexy to stand next to a fixed sewer or repaired bridge. Although in the case of Minneapolis—the city where a major highway

DOI: 10.1057/9781137308733

bridge collapsed on August 1, 2007, killing 13—it still seems ironic that more political capital is gained by funding a new Vikings stadium than by attending to the needs of the streets and sidewalks. Even more ironic, in 2011 a tornado swept though the north side of Minneapolis—a modest income African–American neighborhood—destroying many homes. A year later much of that area was still in ruins while the city of Minneapolis and Minnesota pushed through legislation to help a billionaire sports owner. Why?

Proponents of public investment in sports facilities claim that such development will produce economic gains for a community beyond the sports team (Rosentraub 2008; Rosentraub 2010). However, studies that they tout are often flawed. For example, they usually look only at the positive effects of the stadia and not the negatives, such as offsetting job losses. Macro studies also question the economic impact of sport stadia. Rappaport and Wilkerson report that a study analyzing the 48 metro regions with major league franchises between 1958 and 1987 had no greater increase in growth in personal income per capita than those regions without such teams. In fact at least one study found the growth rates in the former were lower (60). Cities that recently acquired professional sports teams had per capita incomes that fell (Coates and Humphreys 2000).

Literally hundreds of other studies and books by individuals, such as long-time sports economists Arthur T. Johnson in *Minor League Baseball and Economic Development* (1995), Mark Rosentraub in *Major League Losers* (1997), Kenneth Shropshire in *The Sports Franchise Game* (1995), Roger Noll and Andrew Zimbalist in *Sports, Jobs, and Taxes* (1997), and Michael N. Danielson in *Home Team* (1997), reach the same conclusion that public support of professional and minor league sports is a bad investment. In practically none of the cities these studies examined did new sports stadia lead to any significant new private investment or provide for any significant economic benefits to the local economy besides the jobs generated by the initial capital construction of the stadia (Rich 2000: 223–224; Trumpbour 2007: 41). In fact, without prior major private and perhaps non-profit investment, there is no significant public benefit (Rosentraub 2008: 78). More importantly, the new stadia generally were not even profitable or self-financing. Nor could cities point to rising land prices or economic development in the surrounding community. Some like to point to Camden Yards in Baltimore as an example of a stadium revitalizing a community, yet the construction of an aquarium years earlier and other attractions built there earlier had more to do with

DOI: 10.1057/9781137308733

that than a new baseball stadium. On top of which, the Inner Harbor neighborhood still sits on top of one of the city's poorest neighborhoods (Delaney and Eckstein: 32). Even as tourist attractions, the stadia either simply transferred sales from somewhere else, or failed to demonstrate that the local hotels were filled as a result of the sports events (Ford 2003: 199). Finally, in terms of the much-ballyhooed job production, outside of initial construction and the salaries for the players themselves, part time, seasonal, and no-benefits beer and peanut sales jobs were the fare for what the billions of public dollars produced. Overall, as Rappaport and Wilkerson conclude, "Regardless of method, none of the academic studies has so far been able to find significant economic benefits sufficient to justify the large public outlays" (60–61). This conclusion is echoed by Siegfried and Zimbalist (2000:103) who state, "Few fields of empirical economic research offer virtual unanimity of findings. Yet independent work on the economic impact of stadiums and arenas has uniformly found that there is no statistically significant positive correlation between sports facility construction and economic development." But despite this evidence, proponents and politicians carry on.

A second claim to support public investment in a stadium is that retaining a sports team is necessary to ensure that a community remains a first class city because its presence enhances quality of life within it (Feng 2008; Rappaport and Wilkerson 2007: 71; Delaney and Eckstein 2004: 38–40). Would the Twin Cities of Minneapolis and St. Paul (which, besides the Vikings stadium in 2012, also witnessed the State Legislature voting in 2006 to authorize a sales tax worth upwards of $300 million for a new Minnesota Twins stadium) or any city be any worse off by losing a sports team? Without a sports team, most cities would still have parks, museums, zoos, arts facilities, good neighborhoods, schools, and the general quality of life that separates first and second class cities from one another and suburbs. Moreover, if one accepts this logic of sports being necessary to make a city first class, can we say that New York City became second class when the Giants and Dodgers fled for California in the 1950s, or that Los Angeles became second class when it lost the Angels to Anaheim or the Rams to Saint Louis, or that Minneapolis did so when the North Stars hockey team left for Dallas? The answer is obviously no (Delaney and Eckstein 2004: 194–195). There is no indication that metropolitan areas that lost professional sports teams have suffered any measurable loss of quality of life or status (Rappaport and Wilkerson 2001: 75–76).

DOI: 10.1057/9781137308733

Professional sports are only one small piece of what makes a city first class. Moreover, professional sports are also only a small part of the local entertainment puzzle with many consumers often transferring their consumption to other forms of entertainment, including amateur sports, if pro sports are not available. Similarly, sports are even a smaller piece of the local urban economic pie such that its presence or absence is not significant in the face of other features in a thriving and diverse urban area. In addition, with the cost of attending sports events so high, many sporting events are no longer an affordable family entertainment option. According to *Parade* magazine, the average cost for a family of four to attend a football game in 2009 was $412, with it rocketing to $758 to see America's team the Dallas Cowboys (Jenkins 2009). Instead, sports owners look to other corporate interests to buy tickets, thereby making sports an aspect of a city's first class status that is beyond the reach of most of its residents. It is a perk of corporations to wine and dine clients (Delaney and Eckstein 2004: 194–195).

Finally, advocates for publicly funded stadia say that such funding is necessary to maintain owners' profits. Yet who is to say it is the job of the government to ensure private businesses remain profitable? In a free market capitalist society businesses that cannot remain profitable go out of business all the time. Why should a sports facility or team be treated any differently? Further, the issue here is not profitability, but the level or amount of profits the owners want. They would like to make more money and who is to blame them for that desire? However, there are a couple of different issues here. First, many owners say that larger stadia with more seats are necessary if they are to make more money. To support that, owners often trot out attendance figures to show declining profits.

Attendance figures tell only part of the story since they are only a small part of the revenue stream for owners. Revenue from luxury sports boxes, corporate sponsorship and ads, television and radio contracts, and promotions make up a far bigger and more profitable part of what owners receive from their sports adventures (Delaney and Eckstein 2004). Yet even this money is not enough because owners often claim they are not making as much money as other owners and thus, building a new stadium is a key to upping their profits. Owners who claim their teams are less profitable point to richer teams and assert that the building of a new stadium will help them increase profits. Clearly the end result of this "keeping up with the Jones" logic is to constantly push up the average

DOI: 10.1057/9781137308733

profitability of all sports teams such that there will always be some teams below the average demanding financial assistance.

Overall, both the economic evidence and rhetorical argument of sports as defining community to be a winner render public investment in these structures a bad public policy and political myth that deserves to die.

Convention centers

Related to the building of sports stadiums is another edifice often seen as a key to a community's economic fortunes, a convention center. Some contend that *the building of convention and other entertainment centers are successful tools for economic development.*

As noted earlier, the 1989 baseball movie *Field of Dreams* is famously known for a voice echoing "If you build it he will come." While this line inspired legendary baseball player Shoeless Joe Jackson to appear in a ball field in the middle of corn in Iowa, the quote was also supposed to be a mantra to encourage individuals to follow their dreams. However, this line has taken on an even bigger meaning, capturing a theory of urban economic development that places an emphasis upon the building of convention and entertainment centers as a spur to economic development. In the case of the shooting of *Field of Dreams* at Dyersville, Iowa, the ball field has itself become an attraction built or maintained with the hope that they (tourists) will come.

In the past two or three decades many cities have shifted their urban economic development strategies, moving away from housing, office, or retail space construction meant to service its own citizens, to approaches directed to woo tourists and conventioneers to their community (Sanders 2002). As Eisinger (2000: 317) states, the basis of this shift is: "Thus city leaders make entertainment projects a keystone of their urban economic development strategy, hoping that they will generate ancillary development, high employment multipliers in the hospitality and retail sectors, and local tax revenues." Or as Sanders well captures this "if you build it they will come" belief of local officials when it comes to the building of convention space and centers: "[M]ore space will bring more meetings and tradeshows, generating more attendees, dollars, and economic impact" (Sanders 2002: 206). But does this strategy work? Is the building of convention centers or entertainment facilities to promote

DOI: 10.1057/9781137308733

tourism alone going to be the silver bullet that revitalizes an urban core or area economy? The simple answer is no.

There are many reasons why the convention–entertainment center/ tourism strategy has been unsuccessful. First, again as Sanders points out, the massive expansion of convention space in a space of 25 years "from 25 million square feet of space in 1980 to 53.7 million in 2001 to nearly 70 million in 2006" (Sanders, 2002: 195) was premised upon faulty studies and projections regarding the demand for such type of space. All of these studies seemed to assume similarly sustained growth, economic impact, and promises that will flow from tourism. These studies also assume a virtual unlimited growth in convention center demand and the reality is that conventions as activities, especially in a world on the social media, Facebook, and Twitter, are no longer as popular or needed to showcase wares as once they were (Goodman 2009). However, all these studies ignored other issues, such as infrastructure costs and needs (such as for airports) to bring in tourism, or they ignored how the competition from other communities also building similar facilities would drain away demand. In short, Sanders pointed out that the tourism frenzy often relied upon untested claims of development, with studies generally financed and commissioned by downtown tourism bureaus that failed to provide a sound empirical grounding for their rosy projections. These studies, as Sanders points out, were almost verbatim repeated in city after city, ignoring the dilution issues that building multiple conventions centers around the nation would yield. They also ignored that some cities, no matter what, may not simply be the draws for tourism, no matter how much they built.

A second and more fundamental reason behind the failure of the "if you build it" philosophy is premised in the belief that a single factor makes an urban center economically viable. As Jane Jacobs pointed out in *The Death and Life of Great American Cities* (2002) and Larry Ford pointed out in *America's New Downtowns* (2003), cities depend upon a mix of factors to make them thrive, including commercial, retail, housing, office, and other amenities. Jacobs argued that, in part, what makes a city exciting and vibrant is encouraging a mixture of uses that bring people and purposes together. Often times convention centers, built to look like big fortresses, wall off attendees from the rest of the city (Ford 2003: 185). This precludes an integration of the center into the rest of a city's economy. The belief that a city can buy development is incorrect according to Jacobs (1985); no single factor can spur revitalization;

DOI: 10.1057/9781137308733

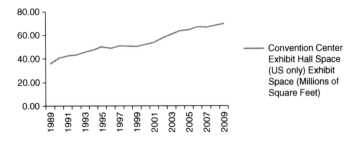

FIGURE 3.1   *Convention center exhibit hall space (US only, millions of sq ft)*
Source: Heywood Sanders personal data.

instead a cluster of factors are critical, including many of those already discussed in terms of what makes an area ripe for business relocation and development.

Tracy (2005) examined the creation of the Orange County, Florida convention center, concluding that it failed to have the economic impact predicted. In searching for answers, one conclusion was that while a lot of money passed through the community, much of it did not stay in Orange County. Often times up to one-third of the conventioneers did not leave the center or stay overnight, thereby mitigating their economic impact. Similarly, places like Niagara Falls receive 12–14 million visitors per year, but despite that traffic, this New York city is able to capture only a small percentage of these individuals and encourage them to spend money in their community. One conclusion to explain all this is that while convention centers and tourist attractions produced a lot of [economic] activity, this is different from economic development. Convention centers, just like enterprise zones or baseball stadiums, shift leisure activities from one place or pursuit to another, but they overall generally fail to produce the desired economic outputs because they are seldom used continuously in the way other facilities are. In many cases, they are often vacant while awaiting the next event. Comparing the multiplier impact of a convention center against building an office or housing which is continuously used, it is no surprise that the former fails to live up to its promises (Goodman 2009).

Finally, again for all of the reasons cited with regard to enterprise zones and baseball stadiums, convention centers and tourism fail as economic development tools. They assume that the tax incentives produce jobs that are cost effective, what results is real and new economic development

DOI: 10.1057/9781137308733

(and not shifts in consumption), or otherwise these projects have better job multipliers or uses of land than rival investments of public dollars (Eisinger 2000; Sanders 1998). Overall, while it might make sense for some cities to pursue a convention center strategy, their effects are eroded when multiple players simultaneously pursue this strategy.

Conclusion

The battle over building sports stadia and convention centers rests upon a dual logic. It is first the logic of "if you build it they will come." It is a belief that the construction of these edifices will have a major impact upon a community. This impact is in terms of creating cities not for residents but for tourists; it is thus a competing vision or bias regarding whom a community serves. As Delaney and Eckstein describe it:

> The more systemic bias is reflected by politicians who genuinely believe that, for their city to survive, they need to transform it into a tourist destination—and they are betting on stadiums to do the job... Professional sports and, in particular, new stadiums are seen as a highly visible way to indicate that a city is still powerful and important (191).

The building of a new sports stadium or convention center is the product of a media–corporate complex, pressuring local politicians into providing a new sports complex to serve their needs. It is less about what the citizens want and more about serving these broader business needs.

But there is also a political logic surrounding stadiums and convention centers. It is logic about a political payoff for politicians. Sure there are the political contributions and securing support from business and perhaps trades unions, but it goes back to the pyramids and Egyptians spoken of at the beginning of the chapter. As business leaders told Delaney and Eckstein: "Enhancing Internet infrastructure, nurturing small business development through seed money, improving education beyond the most basic skills, and developing reliable and affordable mass transit" will have far more and greater impact on an economy than constructing a stadium (192). Yet the authors continue by noting:

> These kinds of improvements, however, are far less sexy, far less visible, and therefore far less attractive to politicians. You often see politicians holding a shovel during a stadium groundbreaking or throwing out the first pitch on opening day. But how many politicians are photographed sitting in the

DOI: 10.1057/9781137308733

driver's seat and opening the doors on one of the city's brand-new-low-pollution buses? (192).

The political payoff in pursuing these follies is far greater than the economic benefits. This is perhaps the main lesson to be learned from this chapter regarding why failed policies and political myths persist.

DOI: 10.1057/9781137308733

4

Welfare Queens, Calculative Criminals, and the Myth of *Homo Economicus*

Abstract: *Laws often embody assumptions about human nature and how people will respond to legislation. Among the most powerful assumptions about human nature is the myth of homo economicus, the economic man, a person who is an omniscient, rational calculator motivated by economic or other similar benefits. Policy makers often assume that specific populations are motivated by certain values or are in possession of knowledge or motives that they actually do not possess. This is especially the case when it comes to welfare recipients and individuals who commit crimes. In general, there is little evidence that people migrate to secure higher government benefits or that most individuals make rational calculative choices when deciding whether to commit crimes.*

Keywords: Welfare migration, repeated offenders, mandatory minimum criminal laws

Schultz, David. *American Politics in the Age of Ignorance: Why Lawmakers Choose Belief over Research.* New York: Palgrave Macmillan, 2013. DOI: 10.1057/9781137308733.

DOI: 10.1057/9781137308733

Introduction

The myth of the welfare queen lives on and hard. In a 1976 speech Ronald Reagan referred to a woman in Chicago on public assistance: "She has eighty names, thirty addresses, twelve Social Security cards and is collecting veteran's benefits on four non-existing deceased husbands. And she is collecting Social Security on her cards. She's got Medicaid getting food stamps, and she is collecting welfare under each of her names. Her tax-free cash income is over $150,000" (Blake 2012). This welfare queen was a glaring indictment of all that was wrong with government and of those lazy individuals—mostly women—who were simply squeezing out more and more children in an effort to avoid work and stay on government assistance.

Americans, by the early 1990s, came to think that welfare—especially a program such as Aid For Families with Dependent Children (AFDC)—was so expensive, wasteful, and corrupt that it was the leading cause of the exploding federal budget deficit. But the reality was that AFDC accounted for less than four-tenths of 1% of the federal budget, few real instances in terms of numbers or dollars were found to be fraudulent, and that most recipients had actually worked within the last two years and few of them were on public assistance for more than a couple of years. Moreover, no one could ever locate Reagan's welfare queen. The reason? She did not exist. She was a myth but nonetheless powerful enough of a myth that it provided the poster child to help change the welfare laws in 1996. This image of the welfare queen as a shrewd, calculating, yet lazy individual seemed odd. She was smart enough to follow welfare laws across the country and migrate to the place with the best benefits. Yet she was also unskilled and not motivated enough to look for real work. The welfare queen was a composite of the best and worst in human nature. Today the welfare queen lives on in references to Barack Obama as the "food stamp president," a shorthand indictment attacking him and the potential turning of America into an entitlement society instead of one premised upon hard work (Blake 2012).

The essence of human nature is a perennial topic of discussion among political philosophers, psychologists, and theologians. At its core the question asks whether by nature human are good or evil with the purpose of ascertaining why there is good and bad in the world. Not surprisingly, there is no firm consensus on who we are as humans.

DOI: 10.1057/9781137308733

In the west, questions about human nature go back to Socrates and the Ancient Greeks including Plato and Aristotle. The Greeks approached these questions by theorizing about human nature. Socrates, Plato, or Aristotle described humans as social creatures with a desire for knowledge and self-perfection. Plato's assumptions about human nature led him in his *Republic* to argue for rule by philosopher kings who were guided by reason. The ideal republic—one where a harmony or balance in the soul matched one's social position or duties—was one where reason as embodied in the philosopher kings ruled the republic.

St. Augustine and many of the early Christian thinkers saw humans as basically base and sinful creatures. Accordingly, their view of government was less noble and optimist than the Greeks'. Government was often viewed as a "punishment and remedy" for human sin. Conversely, medieval Christians such as St. Thomas Aquinas adopted a more Aristotelian view of human nature, reconciling it with Christianity to produce a theory of human nature less base and classical in nature. John Calvin, a sixteenth-century theologian, however, returned to the older Augustinian assumptions about human nature, seeing souls as predestined from birth to be damned or saved. Other theologians adopted varying views on whether humans were good or bad.

In the sixteenth century, the famous British philosopher Thomas Hobbes' *Leviathan* deployed a social contract theory to explain the origins of government. Humans were like machines, and according to Hobbes: "So that in the first place I put for a general inclination of all mankind a perpetual and restless desire of power after power, that ceaseth only in death" (1962: 80). Like John Locke and Jean-Jacques Rousseau, he envisioned that there was once a state of nature before there was government and civil society. This state of nature was a state of war where life, as Hobbes described it, was "solitary, poor, nasty, brutish, and short" (100). It was a war of all against all. Individuals thus formed a social contract in order to protect themselves. What resulted, though, was a social contract to create a near-absolute monarchy. For Hobbes, only a strong king with unlimited powers could keep order, given how contentious human nature was.

Locke, writing in his *Two Treatises of Government*, described humans as basically good but subject to misjudgments in how they enforce and protect their natural rights to property. Government was instituted to help clarify and protect these and other natural rights of individuals. In contrast to Hobbes, though, the social contract that individuals in the state

DOI: 10.1057/9781137308733

of nature execute does not produce a monarchy. Instead, it is more of a limited government subject to what now might be called constitutional constraints. Rousseau, an eighteenth-century French philosopher wrote in his *Discourse on the Origins of Human Inequality* that humans were by nature good but corrupted by society. Or as Rousseau declared in his *Social Contract*: "Man is born free but he is everywhere in chains" (1977: 49).

Finally, among the American Founding Fathers, the best statements regarding the political views and assumptions about human nature and politics that went into the Constitution can be found in the *Federalist Papers*. Government is necessary, as James Madison stated in Federalist 51.

> But what is government itself but the greatest of all reflections on human nature? If men were angels, no government would be necessary. If angels were to govern men, neither external nor internal controls on government would be necessary. In framing a government which is to be administered by men over men, the great difficulty lies in this: you must first enable the government to control the governed; and in the next place oblige it to control itself. A dependence on the people is, no doubt, the primary control on the government; but experience has taught mankind the necessity of auxiliary precautions (Hamilton et al. 1937: 337).

Government is necessary to protect property and check again factions and quarrels that are rooted in human nature, with the Constitution serving as the tool to harness our impulses.

The myth of *Homo Economicus*

There are many other views of human nature beyond those depicted above. Sigmund Freud would, in his various writings, describe humans as guided by the pleasure principle, sexual drives, or a destructive impulse pitting us against ourselves and civilization. B.F. Skinner would depict human nature as plastic, molded by environmental forces, and Abraham Maslow would envision a hierarchy of needs and a drive for self-actualization as explaining human behavior. But beyond all of these pictures of human nature there is another one that defines much of the policy making process—*homo economicus*.

Homo economicus is the man or person of economics. This is the person who is narrowly self-interested, deliberate, and calculating. Consult a variety of classic economic texts and one finds that this person is one who is materialist, wants more as opposed to less happiness, money, or other

DOI: 10.1057/9781137308733

units of please. This is the capitalist person of Adam Smith's *Wealth of Nations* who does not act out of altruism, but instead is a rational calculator. In two of the most famous quotes from this book Smith declares:

> It is not from the benevolence of the butcher, the brewer, or the baker, that we expect our dinner, but from their regard to their own interest. We address ourselves, not to their humanity but to their self-love, and never talk to them of our own necessities but of their advantages.... (1937: 19)
>
> He generally, indeed, neither intends to promote the public interest, nor knows how much he is promoting it. By preferring the support of domestic to that of foreign industry, he intends only his own security; and by directing that industry in such a manner as its produce may be of the greatest value, he intends only his own gain, and he is in this, as in many other cases, led by an invisible hand to promote an end which was no part of his intention. (1937: 335)

The economic person is also god-like. In classical economics, this person is assumed to be omniscient beyond being a pleasure maximizer. In making choices, these economic persons possess a full range of knowledge about the consequences of the different decisions, how it will affect them and others. They are fully calculative, cognizant of all the pluses and minuses of any choice they are to make.

The economic person is a powerful construct. Economists have employed it successfully to reach amazing conclusions about how markets perform. Similar theories of human nature are at the core of organizational and human resources theory, also offering insightful observations that have led to better-run workplaces and companies. Yet the assumptions about the economic person have not gone unquestioned. Nobel Prize winner Herbert Simon questioned the maximizing and omniscient assumptions, suggesting that most decision making takes places in a world of bounded rationality and limited knowledge where actors seek to satisfice as opposed to maximize their choice (Simon 1997). Deborah Stone reaches similar conclusions in contending that real decision making is often limited by narratives, metaphors, interests, and ambiguities (Stone 2001). Charles Lindblom and Edward Woodhouse takes these points even further in arguing that the nature of the policy process, and perhaps decision making in general, is limited to "muddling through" and incremental as opposed to a rational–comprehensive approach (Lindblom and Woodhouse 1992).

The point here is that there are many good reasons to think that while *homo economicus* is a great theoretical construct, it is far more limited in

DOI: 10.1057/9781137308733

its capacity to describe what real people do in real situations. Humans are not computers. They do not have unlimited knowledge of all facts and deliberate in an impassionate fashion. Instead, humans often act impulsively, irrationally, or in ways that display limited awareness about the world around them. Humans are not simply rational robots, but often act out of love, compassion, or even jealously or hatred. In short, humans often act without thinking. Individuals are perhaps as much *homo animosus* (impulsive persons) as *homo economicus*.

But despite this more realistic vision of human nature, too many policy makers somehow believe that individuals are the omniscient calculative creatures of economics, such as the welfare queen and career criminal. Both of these individuals are assumed to be calculative or evil in their decisions to migrate from state to state to collect higher welfare benefits or consider penalties when committing crimes. But the reality is that neither of these individuals generally lives up to the myths surrounding claims about their behavior.

Welfare queens and migration

One policy legend centers on the welfare magnet thesis that contends that *welfare recipients migrate to state simply to seek higher benefits*. In Minnesota, a high-benefit state, elected officials have reached a fever pitch at times in claiming (in visits to my class and in legislative debates) that busloads of individuals in Chicago monthly travel to the state to collect their welfare checks, only to return to Illinois for the duration of the month. As a result, there have been proposals to limit benefits for individuals recently immigrating to the state (Hoppin 2009). Moreover, the lure of the welfare migration thesis was so strong that in 1996 when the federal Personal Responsibility and Work Opportunity Act was passed, it contained a provision allowing states to deny higher benefits to recent migrants to their state for fear that higher benefits would turn some states into welfare magnets. The Supreme Court eventually invalided this provision in *Saenz v. Roe*, 526 U.S. 489 (1999) much like it did 30 years earlier when in *Shapiro v. Thompson*, 394 U.S. 618 (1969) it struck down state laws that also imposed durational residency requirements on individuals before they could receive AFDC payments. Welfare reform in the states produces fears that the individuals migrate on the basis of a rational calculation of benefits. By that, individuals will do a survey

DOI: 10.1057/9781137308733

of welfare benefits around the country and make a deliberate choice to migrate to those with the highest benefits.

What is the reality of welfare migration? Simply stated, it has largely been discredited. For example, the National Research Council found that few AFDC recipients moved between states, and when they did do so, it was not a result of benefit levels (Welfare Law Center 1996: Citro and Michael 1995). Instead, poor people and those on public assistance move from state to state largely for the same reasons as other people. By that, they generally follow overall immigration patterns, moving to states where there are job opportunities, seeking to relocate for family reasons, or looking to get a fresh start in life, just as all other Americans seek to do (Welfare Law Center 1996; Long 1988). Migration patterns in the 1980s and 1990s, for example, demonstrated that the poor tracked towards the Sunbelt states the same as everyone else. These are the states that generally have lower benefits than the high benefit ones in the Midwest and Northeast. Additional studies by Allard and Danziger (1997) and others (Hanson and Hartman 1994; Walker 1994; Levine and Zimmerman 1995; Frey et al. 1995; Schram et al. 1998; McKinnish 2006; Giulietti and Wahba 2012; Bailey 2005; De Jong et al. 2005; Giulietti 2012) also largely discredit the welfare migration thesis as a significant factor affecting the decision of the poor to migrate. These studies examined migration in the United States and across Europe. They researched different types of benefits, and they also compared welfare to other factors such as jobs or wages. They all reached parallel conclusions about the limited impact or non-existence of welfare migration as a significant phenomenon. The claim here is not that welfare migration does not exist at all but that to the extent that it does it is very small in terms of numbers or financial impacts. Studies or claims that welfare is a problem largely ignore how small the migration impact is, how the movement of the poor tracks larger demographic shifts, or misunderstands or characterizes who the poor are and the resources they have to be mobile.

Perhaps the best series of studies in an attempt to document welfare migration and its costs to the state is in Minnesota (typically a high benefit state, especially in comparison to contiguous neighbors), where the state demographer and other offices have examined the issue. A 1987 State Auditor study in Minnesota noted that in 1986 individuals on public assistance both entered and left the state, leaving open questions about the net impact of welfare migration on the state. A 1994 Department of Planning report entitled "Welfare Migrants Add to Minnesota's Rolls"

DOI: 10.1057/9781137308733

found that based on the 1990 census, 4% of all the migrants were on welfare, costing the state approximately $17 million dollars. These welfare migrants cost the state approximately 8% of its total public assistance budget. However, the report was unable to ascertain whether the migrants were on public assistance prior to coming to Minnesota or whether their moving to the state was based upon the welfare benefits or for other reasons such as family or job opportunities.

Another report by the Legislative Auditor (2000) found that migration from other states had in fact increased the state's welfare load, although it could not conclude that individuals came to Minnesota as a result of the state's benefits. Again the report noted that individuals on welfare also left the state but that overall it could not ascertain the net impact of migration. Nor could it, the report noted, state clearly the reasons for the migration, but it did state that "welfare benefits are not the primary reasons for migration by welfare families" (48). However, the overall impact of migration on welfare benefits was small. Finally, a 2000 study by the state demographer, drawing upon census data, also refuted the notion that welfare benefits were a major factor in migration decisions. As the state demographer stated in comments to me (Schultz 2007) once: "In any case, if we were a 'welfare Mecca,' as we have been called, wouldn't the welfare rolls reflect that with an overwhelming number of recipients accumulated over the past nearly 4 decades?" In short, in Minnesota at least, the evidence of welfare migration is negligible at best.

Images of poor people migrating can be found in John Steinbeck's *Grapes of Wrath* or in the 1960s television series *The Beverly Hillbillies*. In the former, Okies move from the dustbowl farms of Oklahoma to seek out the good life in California while in the latter a fictional family moves to that state after striking it rich. Ignored in these depictions are two critical issues. First, the Okies who moved (and they were based on real accounts of migration during the Depression) did so not for welfare benefits but to find jobs. In the case of Jed, Granny, Jethro, and Ellie Mae, characters in the 1960s television show *The Beverly Hillbillies* who strike it rich with oil, they migrated because they were rich and could afford to do so. The reality, as demographers will tell you, is that poor people generally do not migrate because they are too poor to do so. If they do migrate, it is to find work, or be with friends or family or for a host of other reasons. The idea that poor people are capable of doing a rational and comprehensive survey of welfare benefits around the country and therein execute a choice to move to those states with high benefits seems far-fetched.

DOI: 10.1057/9781137308733

Much of the myth of welfare migration is premised upon several questionable assumptions. First, it assumes that the poor are rational calculators who make cost/benefit life style decisions. Second, it assumes they have knowledge about different welfare benefit levels. Third, the benefit differences are enough to outweigh the costs of travel. Fourth, it assumes that these individuals have the resources to migrate. All of these assumptions are questionable. In fact, one could assert that part of what it means to be poor is that one is denied the access to the knowledge and resources to make many of the choices others could make.

Moreover, documented underutilization of many welfare services and programs by eligible individuals questions how knowledgeable most poor people are regarding the availability of governmental benefits, thereby again questioning the omniscience of these people (McKean 2002; Leftin and Wolkwitz 2010; Zedlewski 2002). For example, Zedlewski indicates how only about half of those individuals who qualify for TANF participate in the program, Leftin and Wolkwitz point to 14 million eligible individuals who do not collect food stamps, and McKean points to a 50% utilization rate for stamps, Medicaid, and KidCare (a Chicago area child care program). These studies point to limited knowledge among many individuals—even those who previously participated in some type of welfare program—about many public assistance programs. This limited knowledge thus questions the omniscience and calculating tendency of these individuals, as well as theories that they are migrating across the country to find the state with the most generous benefits.

Overall, the reality of migration is largely confirmed by *The Beverly Hillbillies*—it is the more affluent who move and who are mobile.

Calculating criminals

Welfare recipients are not the only individuals policy makers think are rational calculators. The same assumption is often made about criminals. The assumption is that those who commit crimes, especially the so-called career criminal, do so as a result of a calculative act. Thus, change the penalty to deter crime has led to the belief that *three strikes laws and mandatory minimums are effective deterrents to crime*.

Mandatory minimum penalties are a popular proposal for getting tough on crime. The idea behind them is simple and it is rooted in deterrence theory: Simply increase the sentence for committing a crime and

DOI: 10.1057/9781137308733

the idea is that the average calculating [would-be] criminal will do the math and decide not to break the law.

Mandatory minimums serve as a contrast to indeterminate sentencing. With the latter, a person convicted of a crime such as robbery is sentenced to incarceration perhaps for a period of five to ten years, with a parole board making decisions on release contingent upon the good behavior or rehabilitation of the offender. But skepticism toward judges in the later 1960s and 1970s perceived as being liberal, perhaps because of the image of the US Supreme Court under Chief Justice Earl Warren, led to a backlash against giving judges too much discretion in sentencing. Moreover, the increases in crime in the 1960s led for demands for the criminal justice system to act. Richard Nixon, running for president in 1968 on a platform of "law and order" and also with a promise to get tough on drug usage and urban violence, also tapped into demands to increase penalties for crimes. Part of that strategy included statutory lengthening of prison or jail sentences. Many governors in their states also vowed to get tough on crime. The most prominent of these efforts occurred in New York State in 1973 when Governor Nelson Rockefeller signed into law the toughest drug laws in the country that included a minimum of 15 years to life for the sale or possession of small amounts of marijuana. The Rockefeller drug laws, as they came to be known, set a pattern for other minimum or enhanced criminal penalties across the United States over the next several decades. During the 1980s there was a push toward more determinant sentencing with fixed minimum penalties and a movement away from indeterminate sentencing. Conservative critics of the courts felt judges were too lenient while liberals thought they were too tough or arbitrary when it came to sentencing people of color. Thus the politics of the 1980s came together to produce sentencing guidelines that prescribed specific sentences or for those convicted of crimes. These guidelines included mandatory minimum sentences. But while the idea of mandatory minimums have been around for a while and in part are at the core of determinate sentencing philosophy since the 1980s, the 1990s saw the birth of "three strikes and you're out" laws.

Violent crime was on the rise in the early 1990s, even though the overall crime rate and victimization was still lower than it had been several years before. However, the public rated crime as a major problem, with large majorities supporting enhanced or increased sentences that made it difficult for those convicted of a crime to be paroled. More importantly, corrections research indicated that repeat offenders were a major source

DOI: 10.1057/9781137308733

of crime. By some estimates, "as few as 5 percent of all offenders may account for over half of all robberies and other violent crimes for gain" (Sherman 1983). This research suggested that in many cases simple incarceration for a longer period of time of some habitual criminals would reduce the number of crimes. In addition, there was a growing belief that rehabilitation as a corrections goal had failed (Wilson 1983). Increasing recidivism rates, indicating that larger percentages of inmates were committing crimes and returning to jail, again suggested that incarceration for longer periods of time was a solution to the perceived rising number of crimes and crime rates.

Tougher mandatory minimums were depicted as one way to deter criminals, yet there was little evidence that such laws had much impact. For example, Franklin Zimring and Gordon Hawkins' study of mandatory minimum laws found little impact in deterring crime (Zimring and Hawkins 1995). Studies in Massachusetts, Michigan, Florida, New York, and elsewhere reached similar conclusions (Parent 1997). Good social science evidence was thus available to frame the debates on three strikes to show that mandatory minimums and enhanced penalty laws had little impact on crime. However, while social scientists often like to believe that their research will have policy import, it appears that sentencing studies had little impact on the three strikes debate.

In the early 1990s, a significant portion of public viewed crime as the most serious noneconomic problem facing the country and demands to get tough on it were hardening (Gallup 1993; Gallup 1994). Media accounts of crime on the local news that created the impression of escalating violence on the streets, and the use of the crime by politicians as an election issue fueled this demand. In 1992, President George Herbert Walker Bush ran for reelection calling for the passage of three strikes laws. In 1994 Governor Pete Wilson in California rode to reelection on a get-tough-on-crime platform demanding the passage of a similar law. Finally, several high profile cases, such as the Polly Klass murder by a released criminal in California, also drove the public demand to increase penalties and adopt what would come to be known as three strikes legislation.

Thus, debates about tougher criminal sentences in 1993 came in the context that could be called a frenzied emotional setting. Fears of crime and victimization were running high. Politicians were appealing to this mood, and the media was increasing its coverage of violent crime, rendering the local news as no more than "crime, weather, and sports." Given this climate, three strikes laws were passed by 22 states and the

DOI: 10.1057/9781137308733

federal government between 1993 and 1995. Exactly what offenses were counted as strikes rather than foul balls or how the laws in each case worked varied significantly. However, the idea behind three strikes laws was the same as mandatory minimums. In both cases the assumption first was that individuals who contemplate crimes would be deterred enhanced penalties. In effect, individuals contemplating committing crimes were rational calculators. They would consider the benefits of the crime and weigh it against the potential punishment if caught. Second, if they were not deterred then the longer incarceration periods would serve as punishment or at least keep the bad guys off the street for more years. In either case the belief was that these new enhanced penalty or three strikes laws would reduce crime.

Did the three strikes law decrease crime? Not surprisingly, the answer is no. Zimring et al. (2001) and Schultz (2000a) reached similar conclusions in that the three strikes laws had little deterrent effect and instead produced several unwanted externalities. Zimring et al. (2001) found little evidence of deterrence. For example, there was no evidence that those facing the three strikes laws were less deterred or committed less crimes than those not facing the law. Similarly, this study and Schultz (2000a) noted that crime rates were already going down before the three strikes laws went into effect. Additionally, the spotty use of three strikes in most states questions how much of an impact the laws had on crime rates. Further, comparing three strikes to non three strikes states found no evidence that the former had crime rate decreases greater than the latter. By all statistical measures, three strikes laws did not seem to have much impact on crime rates. Instead, natural downturns in crime as they recessed towards their historical norms, the improvement of the economy, the 100,000 Clinton cops local governments hired with federal money, and perhaps other factors such as decreases in alcohol consumption could account for the decreases in crime. Other studies also reached the conclusion that three strikes and mandatory minimums had little impact on crime (Pew Center on the States 2012; Parker 2012; Kovandzic et al. 2008; Chen 2008: Vitiello 2002; Ramirez and Crano 2003) or that its impact is inconclusive (Schafer 2012). Some such as Harvard researcher Radha Iyengar have even contended that three strikes laws increase crime (Iyengar 2008). Still others assert that these types of laws have done little to mitigate racial disparities in the criminal justice system (Mauer 2010).

Three strikes laws not only had no measurable impact on crime rates but they produced several adverse impacts. For one, as a result of these

DOI: 10.1057/9781137308733

new penalties, the average length of a prison sentence increased by 36% when comparing prisoners released in 1990 as opposed to 2009 (Pew Center on the States 2012). During that time the prison population doubled, with the additional prisoners and time served costing states more than $10 billion beyond what they were already spending on corrections. Some states increased their sentences more dramatically than 36%, with Florida leading at 144% (Pew Center on the States). The cost of incarceration averaged $23,300 per inmate per year.

To pay for the three strikes laws, states had to increase significantly their corrections budgets, often at the expense of education. This was the case in California where the choice of teaching kids how to read or prisoners how to make license plates led to the latter being better funded. Specifically, projections were that by 2012–13 California will spend $15.4 billion on corrections compared to $15.3 on higher education, the former budget growing at an annual average of 9%, and higher education only by 5% (Harris 2007). Per capita, the state spends $8,667 per college student, per year compared to roughly $50,000 per inmate annually according to CNN's Fareed Zakaria (2012). In fact, the spending on corrections in California got so out of hand that in 2011 the U.S. Supreme Court in 2011 in *Brown v. Plata* 563 U.S. __ , 179 L. Ed. 2d 969 (2011) ordered the state to release 33,000 prisoners from their facilities because of severe overcrowding and inadequate mental health care treatment for inmates. There were 156,000 inmates in facilities designed to hold less than half that number.

Three strikes laws also led to states incarcerating individuals for minor crimes or for terms way in excessive of the safety threat posed by these individuals. For example, individuals convicted of property crimes saw a 24% increase in sentence length, from 1.8 to 2.3 years in prison over the past two decades (Pew Center on the States: 3). Finally, three strikes laws led to a potential generation of elderly inmates, replete with medical and health bills that came with them. According to Sharone Story (2011): "As of 2010, 13% of inmates in our prison system were over 55 years old. This number is predicted to increase between four and seven times in the next 20 years, becoming the fastest growing prisoner age group. By 2030, it is estimated that 1/3 of the entire US prison population— currently estimated at 1.6M—will be 55 years or older." Thus, regardless of whether three strikes or mandatory minimums had an impact on crime, the reality is that they were very costly and produced significant unintended consequences that question their effectiveness as a sound criminal justice tool.

DOI: 10.1057/9781137308733

But finally, there is one more criticism of these types of laws that questions the deliberative nature of crime. Three strikes and mandatory minimums are premised upon a deterrence theory of crime which stipulates that knowledge of penalties or consequences (either to you or others) will serve as a deterrent to crime. Specifically, going back to the late eighteenth and early nineteenth century, British philosopher Jeremy Bentham assumed that crime was a rational calculative act that could be deterred if the punishment outweighed the potential benefits of a crime. Conversely, Cesare Beccaria, an Italian jurist writing around the same time contended it was not the severity but the certainty of punishment (Will I get caught?) that deters crime. In either case, crime is a deliberated choice. The reality is that many who commit crimes are not aware of the penalties. Schafer's survey pointed out that large percentages of California offenders were not aware of the three strikes law. Similarly, many crimes are those of passion (second degree murder or manslaughter in some cases) or other crimes involve negligent behavior. The point is that many crimes do not appear to be the product of rational choice but occur with lesser states of mind or intentionality. In some cases potential offenders are not aware of punishments or otherwise do not fit the model of what would be considered to be the type of person who could be deterred by specific punishments or penalties. This limit on the deliberative nature of crime is often levied as a criticism of deterrence theory. Thus, in many cases, potential offenders are not the omniscient rational calculators that policy makers envision. This is not to say that in some cases crime is a calculative act. But the evidence does not bear up that in general those who commit crimes do so with the knowledge and rationality that would affected by three strikes and mandatory minimum laws.

Overall, while sounding like a good idea, three strikes laws strikes out as an effective law enforcement tool. While they may be politically popular and no politician has probably ever lost a race by proposing to get tough on crime, the reality is that mandatory minimums and three strikes laws may be largely and costly ineffective as crime fighting mechanism.

Conclusion

Homo economicus is a powerful tool and construct in economics and social science research. Its use led to important and significant discoveries regarding the operation of social institutions and in many cases it provides clues into explanations of human behavior. But like any tool it

DOI: 10.1057/9781137308733

has its limits and use and it may not be appropriate to use it in specific situations. In the case of explaining the behavior of welfare recipients and criminals, the myth of *homo economicus* is an often misplaced assumption about how people act and make choices. In the case of those seeking public assistance, there is little evidence to support the claim that the poor are the rational calculators fully informed about state welfare benefits and that they have the resources to migrate across states to maximize welfare benefits. Moreover, there is little evidence to demonstrate that welfare migration is a significant public expenditure for states.

There is also little evidence that individuals, especially career criminals, are deterred by enhanced sentencing laws. Almost by definition a career criminal or a repeat offender is one who commits crimes knowing that the act is illegal. If this is the case, then these individuals are aware of the penalties associated with their illegal behavior and they choose to commit crimes. This suggests that these individuals are not making the rational calculations when contemplating their choices. But the reality is that studies suggest that many of the individuals who do commit crimes are not aware of the penalties, again thereby questioning their omniscience and calculating capacities.

The purpose of this chapter is not to argue for abandonment of the *homo economicus* model as a tool of social explanation. Instead its use in this chapter was meant to highlight a powerful set of myths that seems to repeatedly misguide policy makers. All too often, or at least the case with welfare and crime, policy makers assume a level of knowledge and type of behavior among individuals that is, more often than not, incorrect. These faulty assumptions lead to the enactment of policies that either fail in their intended purpose or simply cost taxpayers billions of wasted dollars.

DOI: 10.1057/9781137308733

5
Sending Signals: Illegal Immigrants and Teenage Sex

Abstract: *An important purpose of the law is to communicate to people what is expected of them. Additionally, laws can send signals that sanction or prohibit certain actions. However, for laws to be effective in communicating messages, it requires them to be heard and interpreted by target populations in the ways policy makers intended, yet that is not always the case. This chapter examines whether current laws send signals encouraging foreigners to migrate to the United States, or for teenagers to engage in sexual activity. What it concludes is that there is little evidence to support the beliefs that immigrants are a financial drain on the economy or that the teaching of sex education to teenagers increases their sexual activity.*

Keywords: illegal immigrants, immigration, teenagers, sex education, sending signals

Schultz, David. *American Politics in the Age of Ignorance: Why Lawmakers Choose Belief over Research.* New York: Palgrave Macmillan, 2013. DOI: 10.1057/9781137308733.

Radio antennae and sending signals

Sex, drugs, and rock and roll. A generation of children were raised by parents who feared that rock music lyrics would enrage the former into illegal drug usage and sexual promiscuity. The fear was that rock music, television, and now perhaps Rap music and the Web would expose children to certain messages and encourage illicit behaviors. While such fears are often dismissed as overblown, not everyone would dismiss the idea that Americans are susceptible to peer pressure and social influences.

Sociologist David Riesman once wrote of the change in the American character in his 1950 *The Lonely Crowd*. He was concerned with a sense of conformism that had emerged in the United States and he made a distinction between the inner-directed versus other-directed person. The former followed one's own values while the other sought for behavioral cues in others. In making that distinction he used an analogy— Americans used to be gyroscopes (self-guided or directed) and now they had become radio dishes or antennae in search of signals from others about what to do or say. The power of the "radio dish" analogy resided in depicting how individuals became more attuned to what others thought, thereby determining how they should act or think. In making an argument about the power of public opinion Riesman was not the first. James Madison had noted the power of majority faction in *Federalist Paper* number 10. Alexis De Tocqueville wrote of the tyranny of the majority in *Democracy in America* (1961: 304–308). Thirdly, James Bryce, a famous British observer of the United States wrote, in his 1889 *The American Commonwealth*, of the fatalism of the multitude. According to Bryce:

> This tendency to acquiescence and submission, this sense of the insignificance of individual effort, this belief that the affairs of men are swayed by large forces whose movement may be studied but cannot be turned, I have ventured to call the Fatalism of the Multitude. It is often confounded with the tyranny of the majority, but is at bottom different, though, of course, its existence makes abuses of power by the majority easier, because less apt to be resented. But the fatalistic attitude I have been seeking to describe does not imply any compulsion exerted by the majority. It may rather seem to soften and make less odious an exercise of their power, may even dispense with that exercise, because it disposes a minority to submit without the need of a command, to renounce spontaneously its own view and fall in with the view which the majority has expressed. In the fatalism of the multitude there is neither legal nor moral compulsion; there is merely a loss

DOI: 10.1057/9781137308733

of resisting power, a diminished sense of personal responsibility, and of the duty to battle for one's own opinions, such as has been bred in some peoples by the belief in an overmastering fate. (302).

Bryce saw emerging in the American character deference or demurring to public opinion that seemed quite voluntary and willing. Americans merely had to sense what the prevailing norms were and would conform, without ever so much as the majority really having to act. This was in contrast to the fears of Madison and Tocqueville that misguided majorities would use their numbers illegitimately to suppress the rights of others or to force conformism.

But Madison, Tocqueville, and Bryce seemed to anticipate or see something latent in the American character that Riesman thought had become visible by 1950. Whatever images there were about the myth about the American character of rugged individualism, the reality is that we were less cowboys and more of the "keeping up with the Jones" mentality. We turned to others for choices in terms of fashion, foods, cars, and other consumable choices. We had become a nation more captured by peer pressure and social conformism than by individual behavior. Americans wanted to be team players and not outliers, and we disdained those who were different. From the days of the Salem witch trials in the seventeenth century to the McCarthy communist witch hunts of the 1950s, those individuals who were different were often shunned or condemned. It was thus better to conform to what the majority dictated than to go our own way. Thus, conformism demanded that Americans become radio dishes so as to anticipate and receive the messages sent to by others.

But Riesman's "radio dish" analogy also captures a different aspect of an assumption about humans when it comes to public policy—we are receptive of signals being sent by the government. More specifically, laws or public policies can affect behavior and send signals about what people should do. There is no question that this is a stated aim of the law. Criminal laws are meant to tell people what they should not do. Other laws prescribing rules about the environment, traffic enforcement, and a host of other actions also are in the business of communicating information about acceptable behavior. For laws to be effective, then, they have to be promulgated or made public and announced.

But the concept of policy as sending signals goes even deeper than a general statement that the law communicates a message about acceptable behavior. It is an assertion instead that specific laws are heard by some

DOI: 10.1057/9781137308733

individuals who then act upon them in ways that are consistent with the messages being sent by the policy maker. Policies are radio waves picked upon by individual antennae and people then act upon the signal or message being sent.

A terrific example of this concept of policy as signal sending is drug legalization. The basis for opposing the use of drugs generally rests on one of two grounds. First, there is the moral claim that drug use is inherently immoral or bad because it alters the mind, debases human nature, or reduces the capacity for autonomy. The second claim for opposing the use of drugs is social, arguing that the use of drugs and drug-related activity produces certain costs in terms of deaths, black marketing, and crime. Another variant of this claim is that drug use diminishes social productivity by sustaining bad work habits, or by generating other social costs including increased health care costs. For example, there are good data to suggest that illegal drug use led to increased crime and public health problems. According to FBI Uniform Crime Reports, total state and local drug arrests have increased from 558,601 in 1979 to 1,154,046 in 1988. Additionally, estimates show that there are at least 20,000 premature deaths annually due to illegal drug use, although tobacco and alcohol use account for 400,000 and 100,000 premature deaths respectively (Schultz 1993).

One might concede that use of illegal drugs is bad or that it constitutes a public health problem that needs to be addressed. But having acknowledged this, the question is whether the current practice of drug criminalization is the most effective policy to address this problem. Some have argued no, asserting that legalization of drugs is the answer (Schultz 1993). Yet one argument against the decriminalization approach is the "sending signals" argument. Specifically one major objection to the strategy proposed here is the argument that it would lead to an increase in drug usage and experimentation. Legalizing drugs would send a signal to individuals that drug usage is permissible and therefore more people would use them (Hallfors and Khatapoush 2004).

It is just not clear what impact making drugs legal or illegal has on their usage. Conceivably, making them illegal creates a "forbidden fruit" aura around them that encourages their usage that would be abated by legalizing them. The same might be said for tobacco products and use by teenagers or perhaps for any other products or practices socially shunned. Regardless of the reasons why individuals choose to use drugs, there is little evidence that legalization has resulted in increased usage.

DOI: 10.1057/9781137308733

In the Netherlands, decriminalization of some drugs has not led to an increase in usage or in users trading up from soft to harder drugs (Dennis 1990). Five years after Portugal decriminalized many drugs in 2001, there too was little evidence that it led to increased drug use (Greenwald 2009). Portugal's drug usage rates remain among the lowest in Europe after legalization, while rates of IV drug user infection rates and other public health problems dropped. In legalization of medical marijuana in California, the decriminalization might have changed attitudes toward the drug but there was no evidence of change in its use (Hallfors and Khatapoush 2004). There simply is no real evidence that legalization sends a signal that drugs are permissible and therefore more people use them.

What the drug legalization debate points to is a core assumption often made by many critics of policies. Specifically, the argument will be that if we legalize drugs that will then send a signal to people that their use is not only socially permissible but that the mere legalization will encourage more people to use them. Law can thus induce individuals otherwise not included to do drugs to do them.

There are numerous reasons to why the "sending signals" theory is not valid. One is that this is not in the fact the signal being sent. Decriminalizing drugs does not necessarily mean that people should use them. Lots of behaviors in our society are not illegal yet many individuals opt not to engage in them—such as skydiving or riding motorcycles without helmets. Second, regardless of what signal is being sent, it presupposes that the listener interprets that message that way. People hear what they want or they interpret messages though their own experiences. Whenever someone says that we should not do X because it will send the wrong message to teenagers, the obvious reply is to ask how a 14-year-old would actually interpret that message. Often they would understand the words and messages to mean something rather different from what the message sender intended. This assumes, of course, they are even listening; a questionable assumption held by many parents of teenagers!

Third, there is a big assumption that citizens are even aware of a message. This assumption is similar to the one discussed in the previous chapter regarding knowledge about criminal penalties. Many individuals may be totally unaware of the laws about drugs and therefore may use them at their own risk. The point here is that we live in a loud crowded world with lots of noise around us. Navigating this noise is a problem

DOI: 10.1057/9781137308733

and whatever messaging that is occurring is often hard to discern and sort out. Finally, even if individuals are aware of a message, it may be countered by a competing one that mitigates the first one.

The overall point being made here is that evidence for the "sending signals" argument is non-existent or weak at best. Humans may be susceptible to marketing pressures and advertising as they define consumer choices, but the overall assertion that certain public policies send a signal that encourage certain behavior is vastly overblown. As with the *homo economicus* claim discussed in the previous chapter, the "sending signals" thesis regarding how specific populations respond to government policies seems inaccurate in many cases.

The concept of policy as a behavior inducer is powerful. It is not about assuming that individuals are simply rational calculators as with *homo economicus*. Instead, individuals may act deliberatively or interpret certain policies as endorsing and encouraging specific types of behaviors and actions. Drug behavior is not the singular case where this occurs. Instead, signal sending is a powerful myth in two areas, immigration and teenage sex education. In the case of immigration the assumption is that specific laws or policies in a country such as the United States send signals to individuals in another country that they should migrate illegally or legally to the United States or elsewhere. As a result, immigrants who enter a country become an economic drain and costly to taxpayers. In the case of sex education, the argument is that teaching about sex sends a signal to teenagers that it is permissible to engage in sexual activity and therefore such instruction encourages promiscuity. This chapter examines both of these myths.

Immigration

Immigration seems to be a perennially politically salient issue in the United States. The concern especially seems to be with illegal or undocumented immigrants, with estimates being that there are up to 12 million or more of these individuals in the United States, with the majority coming into the country from across the Mexican border. Stories abound in the news of illegal immigrants making daring treks across the Arizona desert or the Texas Rio Grande River to get into the United States. Or they are packed in trucks or otherwise smuggled into the country via boats or perhaps by even other more outlandish means.

DOI: 10.1057/9781137308733

In order to stem the tide of this illegal immigration numerous proposals have been offered. There is the building of the super high fence between the United States and Mexico. In the past, states such as Texas enacted laws denying children of immigrants funding to attend public school. This law was declared unconstitutional by the Supreme Court in *Plyler v. Doe*, 457 U.S. 202 (1982). In 1994 California voters adopted proposition 187—the Save Our State Act—that would deny all public benefits to illegal immigrants. A federal court eventually struck this law down. States such as Arizona in 2011 passed SB 1070—The Support Our Law Enforcement and Safe Neighborhoods Act—which gave police and authorities in that state increased authority to stop and detain individuals suspected of being illegal immigrants. Also in 2011 Alabama adopted a law requiring police to verify immigration status during routine traffic stops. The law would also require schools to verify immigration status. In 2012 the Supreme Court declared much of the Arizona law unconstitutional. Finally, some have proposed amending the Fourteenth Amendment to prevent the children of illegal immigrants who are born in the United States from receiving automatic citizenship.

During the 2012 Republican presidential primaries the candidates seemed to trip over themselves over who could be tougher on immigration—to the accompaniment of the applause of audience members. At various points New Gingrich and Rick Perry talked of some compassion or route to permit illegal immigrants to become citizens, only to be booed or punished by voters. The Republican nominee Mitt Romney took one of the hardest lines against illegal immigrants, and also suggested that the one solution was for these individuals to "self-deport" themselves, whatever that means. Fears of illegal immigrants has so much overrun the United States in the past few years that the 2010 health care reforms known as Obamacare exempted coverage for these individuals, and the Obama administration has been vigorous in its deportation process, setting an all time annual record of 400,000 in 2011 (Foley 2011).

Why the fear of illegal immigrants? In general, especially in tough economic times, the argument is that *immigration and immigrants take jobs away from Americans and serve as a drain on the economy.* Illegal immigrants are often singled out as competing against American citizens for jobs or that they cost taxpayers money. More specifically, there is a belief that the benefits of citizenship, the free schools, and other programs found in the United States operate like a lure to attract illegal immigrants to the United States much in the same way that supposedly generous

DOI: 10.1057/9781137308733

public assistance programs encourage welfare migration in the United States. Illegal immigrants are depicted similar to welfare recipients as omniscient *homo economicus* making calculated decisions to migrate to the United States. Yet in the case of illegal immigrants, allowing them to work in the United States or get a driver's license, the availability of schooling, health care, and citizenship for children, or even lax enforcement of immigration laws sends a signal to them that they are welcome. Thus, illegal immigrants flock to the United States and something needs to be done to stem this invasion. Now of course for all of the same reasons that welfare migration as a serious problem is a myth, the same types of arguments can be leveled against illegal immigration migration. The claims about immigrants and their omniscience or their awareness of laws are limited. Most poor immigrants lack the resources to migrate or the reasons that they do is hardly sinister—they want to work and have a good life for themselves and their family. The political portrait of these individuals is one that they are all criminals who wish to live on welfare. Thus, on one level the "sending signals" argument seems suspect.

But once one cuts through the stereotypes about immigration, legal or illegal, there are also two specific arguments generally levied against it. One criticism is that immigrants are a net drain on the economy; specifically, they are a bigger drain on taxes and public services than they are overall contributors to the economy. Second, immigrants are depicted as taking jobs away from Americans. What do we know about both of these claims?

First, while acknowledging that immigrants may in some local settings or jurisdictions place some short-term significant burdens upon public services, overall they are net contributors to the economy. Several studies substantiate this point. The *2005 Economic Report of the President* provided a detailed analysis of the impact of immigration upon the United States economy. The report noted that they as a group had up to a $10 billion net positive impact upon the economy (Office of the President 2005: 106–108). The report noted, for example, that while immigrants may be more likely than native born Americans to be on public assistance, the "net present value of immigrants' estimated future tax payments exceeded the cost of services they were expected to us by $80,000 for the average immigrant and his or her descendants" (107). However, with changes in public assistance laws, that figure had been upped to $88,000 (107). While better educated immigrants (high school degree or better) definitely reflect this contribution, even among those not as well educated, the gains from them and their descendants' productivity

DOI: 10.1057/9781137308733

nearly, if not totally, offset the costs they impose upon public services that accrue to state and local governments. Finally, the president's report also provided other documentation regarding the impact of immigrants upon the economy. For example, it noted that immigrants paid Social Security taxes on income of $463 billion dollars (108). Moreover, because illegal immigrants cannot collect Social Security, it is likely that immigrants overall pay more into this government program than they receive from it.

In addition to the President's 2005 report, other studies have noted the net economic benefit of immigrants to the United States. A 1997 National Academy of Sciences study found several net benefits associated with immigration, including a $10 billion net positive impact on the economy. Edmondson (1996) found that: "Illegal aliens in prison cost about $471 million per year, and they consume about $445 million more in Medicaid funds. But these costs are offset by about $1.9 billion in taxes paid by illegals and billions more in consumer spending." Furthermore, the National Academy of Sciences, President's Report, and the Edmondson study, all indicated that younger workers provided for important sources of productivity that also served the economy well. Overall, these and other studies clearly contested the myths that immigrants were a drain on the economy.

In general, broader studies on immigration in the United States also confirm that there is a net benefit of immigrants to the economy (Nadudur 2009). They generally pay more in taxes than they consume in public services. They have provided critical payments to Social Security to help maintain its solvency (Porter 2005). Heidi Shierholz (2010) in *Immigration and Wages: Methodological Advancements Confirm Modest Gains for Workers* found that even native US citizens have seen modest gains in terms of wages as a result of immigration. More importantly, California, Florida, New York, and Texas, the states with the highest immigration, seem to have particularly benefitted from it. Orrenius and Zavodny (2012) reach similar conclusions about the impact on workers while noting that the granting of amnesty to illegal immigrants has benefitted the economy and increased tax revenues to the United States.

The second criticism leveled against immigrants is that they take jobs away from American workers or they negatively impact wages. Again, several studies refuted that (Chomsky 2007). For example, the National Academy of Sciences study found the wage impact to be negligible, while the President's Report found little impact on wages of native Americans

DOI: 10.1057/9781137308733

(105–106). The report also noted and dismissed the argument that immigrants displaced American citizens in the labor market. Instead, they often filled labor gaps abandoned by others, such as farming and agriculture, and they definitely constituted a new source of productive labor particularly at a time when the size of the labor pool from other workers had disappeared.

In addition to the above studies a Pew Hispanic Center (2006) study reached similar conclusions. It compared the economic growth in selected states with high versus low immigration and found no differences in economic growth or in its impact on the labor markets. It also found that there was in fact in 12 states a positive correlation between the growth of immigrant and native-born workers. By that, there was no evidence that in states where more immigrants entered the labor market it depressed the entry of others into work. Finally, even among immigrants who were young and lacking in education, there was no indication that they directly competed against and hurt native-born workers with similar background.

In sum, the evidence that immigrants are financial drains on the economy and that they take jobs away or hurt the wages of native-born workers is wanting. There may be short-term impacts in selected areas where local governments are burdened by immigrants, but both overall and among sport labor markets, it was a myth that immigrants hurt the economy or workers in the way critics of immigration allege.

Teenage sex education

Venturing into social policy where moral and religious issues surface, one finds the discussion of sex education to be a hotbed area of much political myth. Specifically, the argument is that *sex education causes teenagers to engage in sexual activity.*

The United States, like Great Britain, because of their traditionally conservative treatment of human sexuality, has had a history of difficulty with legislation dealing with contraception and birth control. At the top of the list in this area is controversy over the teaching of sex education in schools. Among the objections raised is the assertion that the teaching of sex education, or about birth control, for example, will lead to increased sexual curiosity and therefore activity among juveniles. Thus, if one wishes to decrease sexual activity among minors, or at least

DOI: 10.1057/9781137308733

sexually transmitted diseases, then teaching about sex is exactly the opposite policy that should be adopted. Instead, one should not discuss the issue (at least in school) or if it must be discussed, abstinence-only should be the message that is conveyed to teenagers. One quick response often offered here is that minors are going to engage in sexual activity no matter what, so one might as well tell them the way to do it safely. This response, however, ignores the argument regarding the alleged link of sex education to sexual activity.

Is there a linkage? Does sex education cause teenagers to engage in sexual activity? Is the teaching of sex in school sending signals to teenagers encouraging them to be more sexually active? In general, scientific research has demonstrated that sex education for minors does not increase sexual activity (Pleck 1992; Sulak et al. 2006; Kirby 2002; Oettinger 1999; Baldo 1998; Furstenberg et al. 1997; Wellings et al. 1995; Wymelenberg 1990; Bearman and Bruckner (2001); Bruckner and Bearman (2005); Dailard (2000); Kirby (2001); Satcher (2001)). More specifically, AIDS and sex education lead to a decrease in sexual activity (Pleck 1992). Increased sexual knowledge has resulted in a decrease and delay in sexual activity (Sulak et al. 2006). School-based clinics and school condom-availability programs do not increase sexual activity (Kirby 2002; Edwards et al, 1980; Kirby et al., 1993; Kirby et al., 1991; Kisker et al., 1994; Newcomer et al. 1996; Zabin et al., 1986). A World Health Organization study found that sex and AIDS education did not lead to sexual activity (Baldo 1998). Condom access did not lead to increases in sexual activity (Furstenberg et al. 1997), and sex education did not lead to an increase in sexual activity or the lowering of the age for first sexual experience (Wellings et al. 1995). Overall, the evidence is solid, numerous studies have repeatedly refuted the claims that increased sexual knowledge increases sexual activity. Instead, studies have pointed to a decrease in teenage pregnancy in the United States over the past couple of decades (to the lowest level in seven decades) that can be attributed to increased knowledge about birth control and contraception use and not to abstinence education (Hamilton and Ventura 2012; Martinez et al., 2011). There is no good evidence that the teaching of sex education has promoted teenage sexual activity. Conversely, this claim does not refute assertions that teaching abstinence is an effective tool at decreasing sexual activity and in fact in some situations it might be (Stein 2010). Instead, the claim here simply is that the teaching of sex education does not do that either.

DOI: 10.1057/9781137308733

The discussion of sex education and minors here is meant to highlight what appears to be a broader myth or error that many policy makers make. That is, often times legislation is debated or discussed and the argument against, or for it, is something to the effect that "it will send the wrong message to children." Quite simply and for the most part, most adults have no idea what messages are being heard by children and how they are being interpreted. As a result of work by Jean Piaget and other developmental psychologists, we know that children interpret and organize the world differently from adults. Whatever messages adults may think policies are sending is often mere conjecture. Instead of guessing what message a teenager may be receiving, go ask one...or several! Perhaps with the exception of adults at the cigarette and tobacco companies responsible for Joe Camel, few probably understand what children are learning from adult messages. This suggests that unless one is prepared to document from surveys or other empirical means what a specific message may mean to children if they are listening, this objection to policy making needs to be banished.

Conclusion

Major myths in the making of policy often centers on visions of human nature and psychology. Whether it is the rational calculator of *homo economicus* discussed in the previous chapter or the radio antennae model of the "sending signals" theory examined here, these constructs of human nature seem to assume humans as some sort of omniscient and attentive creature that acts either rationally or conversely, divine specific messages from policies enacted by the government. Yet this is far from the case when specific policies are examined. Instead, much of the debate around issues such as immigration and teenage sexual activity (and welfare and crime) are largely poorly informed or premised on assumptions about human behavior that are just not accurate. Moreover, and this is the main argument of this chapter, it just does not appear to be the case that many of the assumptions surrounding immigration and the teaching of sex education are correct. These faulty assumptions question not only the substance of the policies in these areas but also the logic policy makers employ in these and in other areas when it comes to interpreting and regulating human behavior.

DOI: 10.1057/9781137308733

6
Democracy Is the Worst Form of Government

Abstract: *Americans hate politics and government, often seeing both as corrupt. Two areas of concern seen as contributing to this corruption are voter fraud and career politicians. Voter photo identification and term limits have been proposed to address both of these issues. Yet there is little evidence that voter fraud is generally a major problem that has affected the outcome of elections and which could be prevented by voter identification. Additionally, terms limits generally have not worked as advocates had hoped and instead of weakening the power of veteran legislators, they have strengthened the influence of lobbyists and not done much to reduce political gridlock or change politics.*

Keywords: Voter fraud, voter identification, career politicians, term limits, political gridlock

Schultz, David. *American Politics in the Age of Ignorance: Why Lawmakers Choose Belief over Research.* New York: Palgrave Macmillan, 2013. DOI: 10.1057/9781137308733.

> "Don't vote—it only encourages them."
>
> Jack Paar

Winston Churchill once quipped that: "Democracy is the worst form of government, except for all other forms." The former British prime minister's comment well captures views in the United States toward government. Americans have a love–hate relationship with politics and politicians. Politics seems to be one of the great conversational sports in the United States where everyone seems to enjoy talking about it, while at the same time Americans like to complain about government inefficiency and corruption. Americans take pride in having the greatest democracy in the world, yet the reality is that voter turnout in the United States compares poorly to other major free societies. While in recent years presidential voter turnout has inched back up to around 60%, this turnout pales in comparison to 70% plus in many western European democracies. As recently as 1996 Bill Clinton was reelected president with a turnout of less than 50%.

The contradictory images of American politics dates perhaps to the constitutional origins of the country, if not earlier. Within the American political culture is a belief that the people and popular opinion should rule. As James Madison declared in *Federalist* 49 "all government rests on opinion" (Hamilton et al. 1937: 329). But he feared in *Federalist* 10 that should that opinion turn dark, it would become a majority faction threatening individual liberty and republican or popular government. Similarly de Tocqueville's *Democracy in America* described tyranny of the majority too as a threat to individual liberty. The task was thus how to let the people rule but check the passions and excesses that flowed from popular sovereignty. Additionally, while James Madison and other constitutional framers placed faith in elected leaders filtering the passions of the people, there was also a concern that left unchecked, these rulers would become a threat to liberty. As Madison stated in *Federalist* 51:

> But what is government itself, but the greatest of all reflections on human nature? If men were angels, no government would be necessary. If angels were to govern men, neither external nor internal controls on government would be necessary. In framing a government which is to be administered by men over men, the great difficulty lies in this: you must first enable the government to control the governed; and in the next place oblige it to control itself. (337)

DOI: 10.1057/9781137308733

According to Madison, government must control the people and vice versa. There is a constant fear that without the proper checks corruption would wreck havoc, and undermine the government and liberty.

Voting and elections are major tools to ensure an accountable government that reflects the views and opinions of the people. It is almost a bedrock principle of American politics that our government is premised upon consent of the governed and majority rule. Yet what if voting and elections do not work? What if, for example, persons not eligible to vote—such as non-citizens—cast ballots, or what if someone impersonates another? Would majority rule be properly served or expressed? Or what if despite elections, some officials are so entrenched in office that somehow the voters cannot remove them, where is the accountability or ability of the majority to get its way? These are clearly serious concerns. Events in the news point to flawed elections around the world where the votes are rigged. Free and fair elections are necessary if a democracy is to work properly.

Two fears that permeate American politics are that voter impersonation is a widespread problem in the country that affects the outcome of elections, and that incumbents have so entrenched themselves in office that they cannot be removed, even by elections. These two fears have translated into two policy prescriptions. First, that voter photo identification is necessary to address this widespread fraud. Second, that term limits, at least for legislative bodies, will dismantle incumbent advantages, break their ties to special interests, and discourage career politicians. This chapter investigates these two policy concerns, asking how widespread in-person voter fraud at the polls is, and also what impact term limits really have in terms of breaking special interest politics or changing how legislators act. What the evidence will show is that current proposals for voter identification are a solution in search of a problem and that term limits fail to live up to their promise in terms of altering politics along the lines that many of its advocates desired. Thus, both voter fraud or photo ID and term limits are two additional failed policies or myths that seem to be guiding policy deliberations in America now.

Voter fraud

Bush v. Gore 531 U.S. 98 (2000) was a controversial landmark decision in which the Supreme Court halted the recount of ballots in the 2000

DOI: 10.1057/9781137308733

Florida presidential election and effectively resolved the outcome of the election in favor of George Bush over Al Gore. But the events surrounding this decision and the presidential voting in Florida raised calls from both Republicans and Democrats that voter fraud affected the outcome of the election. Since Florida 2000, concerns have been raised, often in very close elections (and usually by the losers), that there is wide-spread voter fraud in the United States affecting the outcome of elections and something needs to be done to address this fraud. Thus, increasingly one policy proposal trotted out is to argue that *voter photo identification is needed to address widespread election fraud in the United States.* But the question is how significant is in-person voter fraud in the United States and will voter ID be able to prevent it? The simple answer is that voter fraud is virtually an insignificant problem in the United States with the chances of one being struck by lightning greater than voter fraud affecting the outcome of an election. This means that voter ID is a remedy in search of a problem.

So what do we really know about voter fraud? If voter fraud is not a significant problem, why the demand for voter ID? To answer these questions it is necessary to understand something about the legal struggle for the right to vote.

Americans thus have a long history involving a struggle to secure a right to vote. The country has moved a long way from the days when only white, Protestant, property-owning males of age 21 or more were the only ones who voted. When it comes to voting and voting rights, American history is marked by two traditions (Keyssar 2000). One expresses a continuing expansion of the formal right to vote beyond that found at the time of the framing of the Constitution when only white male property owners of Protestant faith and specific age and citizenship had franchise rights under the Constitution (Stephenson 2004: 41–64; Keyssar: xvi). As former Supreme Court Justice Thurgood Marshall aptly put it:

> For a sense of the evolving nature of the Constitution we need look no further than the first three words of the document's preamble: "We the People." When the Founding Fathers used this phrase in 1787, they did not have in mind the majority of America's citizens. "We the People" included, in the words of the Framers, "the whole Number of free Persons." On a matter so basic as the right to vote, for example, Negro slaves were excluded, although they were counted for representational purposes at three-fifths each. Women did not gain the right to vote for over a hundred and thirty years (Marshall 1987).

DOI: 10.1057/9781137308733

According to Marshall, it would take "several amendments, a civil war, and momentous social transformation" before the right to vote began even to remotely approximate the promises that "We the people" held out.

But while one American tradition is marked by an expansion of franchise, Alexander Keyssar notes another tradition characterized by efforts to deny the right to vote. There are repeated periods in American history where efforts have been made to disenfranchise voters or to scare them away from the polls. For example, after the Civil War many in the South used Jim Crow laws, poll taxes, literacy tests, grandfather laws, and not so subtle means, such as lynchings, cross burnings, and other techniques to prevent newly freed slaves from voting (Woodward 1974).

In the late nineteenth and early twentieth centuries, bans on fusion tickets (multiple or cross party endorsements of the same candidate), instant runoff voting, proportional voting, and other so-called reforms were instituted to discourage immigrants and urban poor from voting (Keyssar: 127–141). In both cases, the pretext for the suppression of voting rights was the claim of fraud (Keyssar: 159–162; Stephenson 143–154); the efforts resulted in significant drops in voter turnout. This was America's first great disenfranchisement.

Now, claims about voter fraud and efforts to deter it with voter ID are potentially part of a second great disenfranchisement that is afoot across the United States. This time the tools are not literacy tests, poll taxes, or lynch mobs, but rather the use of photo IDs when voting. Members of the Republican and Democratic parties have dueled over proposals to make voting requirements more stringent or more relaxed since the 1980s (Keyssar: 314), but the real battle began in the Florida 2000 and Ohio 2004 presidential contests (Fitrakis et al. 2006). It continues today as allegations of fraud in both of those states have led to efforts to increase voting requirements. Following the disputed 2000 presidential election in Florida, Congress enacted the Help America Vote Act (HAVA) as an effort to improve voting, but it came with some picture ID requirements. According to the *Wall Street Journal* at least half of the states have added additional alleged anti-fraud mechanisms since HAVA (Conkey 2006) and several states, including Arizona, Georgia, Indiana, Michigan, and Missouri, have imposed photo ID requirements to vote at the polls. Proponents justify these efforts on the premise that voter fraud is real and that these measures are needed to control it. As each new presidential and congressional elections approach, claims of voter fraud

DOI: 10.1057/9781137308733

and the issue of photo identification are heating up. Fraud has become a partisan issue, with Republicans appearing to believe in its existence and support voter IDs, with Democrats generally denying it as a serious issue and opposing the new voting requirements as a means of suppressing turnout to the advantage of the former (Liptak 2007).

But what do we really know about voter fraud? Is there widespread voter fraud in United States that is affecting the outcome of elections? The answer is not easy, given that there are no comprehensive peer-reviewed studies examining voting fraud in the United States. Even the United States Election Assistance Commission acknowledged this (2006). For the most part, most of the stories about fraud are just that—stories and anecdotal tidbits of information not well corroborated or systematically studied. On top of that, the term "voter fraud" is vague. Lorraine Minnite, who has studied the issue perhaps as well as anyone, seeks to define voter fraud by drawing upon a broader Department of Justice definition that states that election fraud is the "conduct that corrupts the process by which ballots are obtained, marked, or tabulated; the process by which election results are canvassed and certified; or the process by which voters are registered" (Minnite 2007b: 6).

Minnite locates voter fraud as a subcategory of this broader concept of election fraud, defining it as the "intentional corruption of the electoral process by voters" (2007b: 6). She wishes to distinguish this form of fraud from that which takes place at the hands of election officials, parties, candidates, and others who are involved in election administration and political campaigns. Minnite's definition of voter fraud will be used here. However, it is important to note that besides voter fraud, there is "election official fraud." The latter will include situations in which election officials or parties other than voters falsely register or permit ineligible individuals to vote, engage in vote buying or swapping, or engage in other forms of vote suppression or manufacturing.

Even within the category of voter fraud it is important to realize that a host of activities can be included under this term. Voter fraud could include intentional efforts to register falsely to vote or actually to vote falsely. Allegations of voter fraud include claims that illegal immigrants, ex-felons, and impersonators are stealing the identities of others, including the dead, in order to vote illegally. Voter fraud could also take place in several venues, such as at the polls on election day, in completing an absentee ballot, or in completing the paperwork necessary to register to vote. Given these distinctions, the evidence is clear: there is little

DOI: 10.1057/9781137308733

systematic or widespread voter fraud in the United States that is changing the outcome of elections. This is at least true among the types of
fraud that voter ID laws are meant to address.

The three most persistent claims of voter fraud come from the *Wall
Street Journal's* John Fund, a report from the Senate Republican Policy
Committee in Congress, and the Carter–Baker Report. There have
been other allegations of voter fraud but none rising to the level of a
systematic study of the topic. Fund's *Stealing Elections: How Voter Fraud
Threatens Our Democracy* (2004) calls for mandatory photo identification
to be displayed when voting in-person at the polls because of widespread
fraud occurring in the United States. The concern is allegations of voter
impersonation at the polls. Yet what evidence exists that voter fraud of
this type is rampant? There is little systematic evidence offered here.
Stealing Elections draws upon interviews around the country to whip up
hysteria that droves of dead people, illegal immigrants, vote brokers,
and ex-felons are cheating their ways into the voting booths, stealing
elections from honest decent Republicans, and diluting the votes of red,
white, and blue Americans. But when the smoke of Fund's allegations
clears, there is little fire of voter fraud, at least of the kind he alleges.

For example, Fund alleges that the Florida 2000 presidential election
demonstrated "sloppiness that makes fraud and foul-ups in election
counts possible...." (3–4). Even if one accepts all of his comments as true,
the sloppiness he alleges is not voter fraud; the problems are with election
officials. Fund also alleges that "lax standards for registration encouraged
by the Motor Voter Act have left the voter rolls in a shambles in many
states" (25). Again, this mere allegation does not document which states,
what shambles means, how the problems affect voting, or whether those
problems constitute voter fraud. *Stealing Elections* is rife with these types
of unsubstantiated allegations of election fraud, let alone voter fraud,
that he claims have actually risen to a level that affects elections. Fund
seems only to offer anecdotal evidence that election officials have erred
in letting some individuals register when they should not have, or that a
few persons have tried to vote twice in the same election, such as showing up to the polls to vote after forgetting they voted by absentee ballot.
Fund, in an op-ed (2007), seems not to have learned the lessons of his
ways. In that *Wall Street Journal* essay he referenced a felon named Ben
Miller in Florida who voted illegally for the past 16 years and mentioned
that in the Florida 2000 election there were 5,643 voters' names that
"perfectly matched the names of convicted felons." However, what Fund

DOI: 10.1057/9781137308733

does not say or apparently seek to investigate or prove is whether Ben Miller knew he was ineligible to vote or whether election officials incorrectly registered him. In terms of the 5,643 names, Fund fails to show that in fact these individuals were barred from voting or that they were doing anything wrong. Ex-felons, after all, are not barred from voting in all states and in all circumstances as Fund's insinuations would imply. For the most part, Fund's allegations are based upon rumor, half-truths, and innuendos that fail the test of any valid social science study.

A second report by Senate Republican Policy Committee entitled *Putting an End to Voter Fraud* (2005) asserts that "[v]oter fraud continues to plague our nation's federal elections" (1). The basis of its allegations rests in assertions that the National Voter Registration Act of 1993 (The Motor Voter Act) has made it difficult to maintain accurate lists to keep people from voting illegally (5), that non-citizens are voting illegally (7), and that there may be risks associated with early and absentee voting (8). Again, little evidence of voter fraud, either of a substantive or systematic nature, is offered. For example, the report cites allegations of illegal voting in the 2004 Wisconsin presidential elections (7), but provides no firm numbers to show whether the allegations are true or significant. In terms of the threat of non-citizens voting, the report mainly references efforts in many jurisdictions to change the law to allow non-citizens to vote legally.

Those who argue that there is widespread voter fraud that requires new measures like voter IDs to combat fraud often cite a third report entitled *Building Confidence in U.S. Elections: Report of the Commission on Federal Election Reform*, which was chaired by former president Jimmy Carter and former Secretary of State James Baker ("Carter–Baker Commission"). The report asserts that: "[W]hile election fraud is difficult to measure, it occurs" (45). Proof of this assertion is citation to 180 Department of Justice investigations resulting in convictions of 52 individuals from October 2002 until the release of the report in 2005 (45). Yet while the Carter–Baker Commission called for photo IDs, it also noted that: "[T]here is no evidence of extensive fraud in U.S. elections, or of multiple voting, but both occur, and it could affect the outcome of a close election" (45). As with other studies, absentee voting is singled out as the place where fraud is most likely to occur, followed by registration drives by third parties (46).

Empirical evidence supporting the Carter–Baker Commission findings of fraud is scant at best. As noted, the report's conclusion is that fraud is

DOI: 10.1057/9781137308733

not extensive, but when the report does cite to support its claims, it references newspaper articles and other accounts that are not corroborated or subject to critical analysis (18, 73). As the Brennan Center stated in its analysis and response to the Cater–Baker call for a voter photo ID: "[T]he Report attempts to support its burdensome identification requirements on four specific examples of purported fraud or potential fraud. None of the Report's cited examples of fraud stand up under closer scrutiny" (Weiser 2005: 9). Even if all of the documented accounts of fraud were true, the Brennan Center points out that in the state of Washington, for example, six cases of double voting and 19 instances of individuals voting in the name of the dead yielded 25 fraudulent votes out of 2,812,675 cast—a 0.0009% rate of fraud. Also, assume the 52 convictions by the Department of Justice are accurate instances of fraud. This means that 52 out of 196,139,871 ballots cast in federal elections, or 0.00003% of the votes were fraudulent. While critics might assert that these cases represent only the tip of known cases of a fraud iceberg, it is important to underscore that the prosecutions occurred on the heels of a Justice Department taking an aggressive stance on this crime (Lipton & Urbina 2007). One is in greater danger of being hit by lightning than an election being affected by fraud.

While studies seeking to prove voter fraud offer a paucity of evidence, studies reaching the opposite conclusion are more plentiful. The U.S. Elections Assistance Commission ("EAC") undertook a broad review of literature and expert interviews on what was then known about voter fraud when the EAC was operating, creating the report *Election Crimes: An Initial Review and Recommendations for Future Study* (2–3). It concluded that "[m]any of the allegations made in the reports and books ... were not substantiated[,]" even though they were often cited by many parties as evidence of fraud (16). The report held that the same was true regarding media accounts and that even stories about prosecutions lacked reliable follow up (16–19). Overall, the report noted that while "impersonation of voters is probably the least frequent type of fraud because it is the most likely type of fraud to be discovered, there are stiff penalties associated with this type of fraud, and it is an inefficient method of influencing an election" (9). Instead of impersonation, absentee ballot voting was described as most susceptible to voter fraud, but, even with it, the EAC called for more statistical analysis to determine its seriousness.

However, even as this version of the EAC report downplayed voter fraud while calling for more study of the subject, the original draft was

DOI: 10.1057/9781137308733

more conclusive in dismissing allegations. According to the *New York Times*, "[A] federal panel, the Election Assistance Commission, reported last year that the pervasiveness of fraud was debatable. That conclusion played down findings of the consultants who said there was little evidence of it across the country, according to a review of the original report ... obtained by *The New York Times* and reported on Wednesday" (Lipton & Urbina 2007). As reported in the *New York Times*, experts hired by the EAC to consult with them largely found that mistakes and errors on the part of election officials, as well honest mistakes by voters, have caused some problems. Yet overall, according to Richard G. Frohling, an assistant United States attorney in Milwaukee: "There was nothing that we uncovered that suggested some sort of concerted effort to tilt the election...." (Lipton & Urbina 2007). In effect, while the final version of the EAC report seemed tentative in dismissing fraud as a phenomenon, the experts and perhaps even the original version of the report were even more conclusive on this point.

Lorraine Minnite has conducted several studies on the extent of voter fraud in the United States. One of those studies cites statistics provided by the Department of Justice that indicate that between 2002 and 2005, when the Attorney General made election fraud and corruption a priority, only 26 individuals were convicted or pled guilty to illegal voting, including five who could not vote because of felony convictions, 14 non-citizens, and five who voted twice in the same election (2007a). During that same time period, another 14 individuals were prosecuted by the Justice Department but not convicted. Minnite has also noted how states have heavily criminalized voter fraud, and local law enforcement officials do not seem to be shying away from election fraud issues as a result of a lack of desire, ability, or resources to combat fraud. Moreover, when Minnite examined the often told allegations of illegal voting or registration in Wisconsin during the 2004 presidential race, she found that either the individuals did not know they voted illegally, that the stories were later recanted, or that prosecutions (a total of three) were dropped due to a lack of evidence. Overall, Minnite's conclusion is that voter fraud allegations are really partisan Republican efforts to suppress voting.

Other studies have reached similar conclusions about the lack of voter fraud. While some, such as the Republican Senate Policy Committee, express concern that the Motor Voter Act is a potential source of voter fraud, an EAC report on the law's impact did not discuss fraud (2007). In the report, voter fraud is not discussed in the section on voter verification

DOI: 10.1057/9781137308733

(12). In fact, the report seems to suggest that states have this issue under control. The problem getting the most attention is removal from voter rolls for non-voting (11). An Office for Democratic Institutions and Human Rights report found only isolated reports of voter fraud or impersonation (2007). Additional analysis on the impact of the Motor Voter Act by Jonathan E. Davis (1997), the Carter–Baker report (Overton 2007), and a Rutgers University study of the impact of provisional voting procedures as outlined in the Help America Vote Act of 2002 (Eagleton Institute 2005) also found little, if any, evidence of fraud in American elections.

Claims of fraud persist despite these studies. In the 2008 Minnesota Senate race, the 312-vote margin of victory (out of nearly 3 million votes cast) that Al Franken had over Norm Coleman was marred by allegations of voter fraud, as was the 2010 Minnesota governor's race where Mark Dayton defeated Tom Emmer by approximately 9,000 votes. Wisconsin in 2011 passed voter identification laws, which were subsequently enjoined by state courts as possibly unconstitutional. South Carolina and Texas sought to implement voter identification but the U.S. Justice Department halted their enforcement as possible violations of the Voting Rights Act because of the potential impact such laws may have upon minority voters. Up into the 2012 election season fears of election fraud persisted. Governor Rick Scott in Florida ordered a purge of voter lists in that state because of fears that non-citizens may be voting. At least for the foreseeable future, allegations of voter fraud will taint any close election in the United States.

Supporters of voter identification assert that despite the relative absence of widespread voter fraud, it nonetheless exists. Perhaps the best statement regarding the empirical debate over voter fraud is by Judge Richard Posner who wrote the majority opinion in Seventh Circuit *Crawford v. Marion County Election Board* (F.3d. 949 (7th Cir. Ind. 2007)), which upheld the state's voter ID law. He argues:

> Without requiring a photo ID, there is little if any chance of preventing this kind of fraud because busy poll workers are unlikely to scrutinize signatures carefully and argue with people who deny having forged someone else's signature.
>
> But the absence of prosecutions is explained by the endemic underenforcement of minor criminal laws (minor as they appear to the public and prosecutors, at all events) and by the extreme difficulty of apprehending a voter impersonator. He enters the polling place, gives a name that is not his

DOI: 10.1057/9781137308733

own, votes, and leaves. If later it is discovered that the name he gave is that of a dead person, no one at the polling place will remember the face of the person who gave that name, and if someone did remember it, what would he do with the information? The impersonator and the person impersonated (if living) might show up at the polls at the same time and a confrontation might ensue that might lead to a citizen arrest or a call to the police who would arrive before the impersonator had fled, and arrest him. A more likely sequence would be for the impersonated person to have voted already when the impersonator arrived and tried to vote in his name. But in either case an arrest would be most unlikely. (953)

For Posner, fraud detection is difficult and the costs associated with prosecution are high, thereby yielding minimal incentives to prosecute.

Posner parallels voter fraud to littering, contending that both are difficult to detect (953). Others, such as Brad Smith, former chairman of the Federal Election Commission, similarly highlight the few reported or prosecuted instances of fraud as perhaps indicative of a more extensive problem (although he does admit that fraud is not extensive). His parallel is to vehicular moving violations: "[T]he typical speeding ticket or even DWI is usually indicative of numerous other, unreported events of the same nature. But surely that is true of voter fraud as well" (Smith 2010).

What does all this mean for voter fraud studies? Who is correct? Why, despite the evidence, do claims about voter fraud persist? In part the answer is that the assertions have not been framed as testable or empirical assertions but instead lobed as political bombs. They are cries to motivate a political base or delegitimize the victory of an opponent one does not like. The arguments, even in such places as the online Election Law Listserv, a forum for election law professors, litigators, and politicos, are cast more as ideological positions by partisans than it is by political scientists framing the debate as a social science question.

To resolve the debate it is important to restate claims about voter fraud in terms of testable (falsifiable) claims. The arguments need to be framed in ways that allow it to be tested. We need to be able to generalize from specific instances of fraud to be able to make broader assertions. Are the few instances that are detected a good sample indicative of a broader population of fraud?

What would be a testable voter fraud claim? As one reads those who assert its widespread existence, several claims seem to emerge. First, we

DOI: 10.1057/9781137308733

do not know the extent of fraud since we do not have voter photo ID. This claim recognizes the lack of evidence and asserts the solution is to institute photo ID. Once in place, it would reveal the extent of attempted fraud. However, for those who also contend the fraud exists, once photo ID is instituted, the lack of increase in detected fraud is proof that the additional measure (photo ID) works to prevent fraud. While this may be true, proponents cannot have it both ways. The arguments are a circular logic at best; they both cannot be true at the same time. Moreover, they may not be empirical and testable propositions capable of falsification.

First, think about what would be valid evidence to document fraud. Paul Wyckoff describes a hierarchy of empirical evidence based on its reliability (2009: 18–19). At the top of the evidence chart are controlled experiments where studies can manipulate critical variables and test them (22–24). At the bottom are case studies and anecdotes where there is almost no ability to test and verify facts and control variables (18–19). A critical issue in evaluating qualities or types of evidence is the ability to generalize from them to reach some larger propositions (18–19). In other words, do the case studies, anecdotes, or experiments serve as good samples that represent the larger population? Generally simple stories or anecdotes are weak evidence because one cannot easily use them to make inferences about broader trends or populations unless other evidence or reasons are offered to support drawing broader conclusions. Additionally, simple stories, unless corroborated, are like hearsay and are unable to withstand truth tests to ascertain their credibility and reliability.

This is an important point because for the most part the quality of the evidence offered by Fund and others is anecdotal. Thus, the first major problem with John Fund and arguments regarding voter fraud is the quality of the evidence. It is unsubstantiated and of the lowest quality. Its ability to be examined and then generalizations drawn from it are questionable. Those who believe voter fraud exists and is widespread generally references stories alleging felons, illegal aliens, or others voting or casting multiple votes. The stories quickly make the news but then upon later examination they are rejected as false or fail to secure corroboration. For example, claims of voter fraud in the 2004 Wisconsin presidential contest failed to produce evidence and prosecution (Schultz 2008a: 497).

A second problem with voter fraud arguments is fashioning allegations into testable empirical propositions. Again, if good social science

DOI: 10.1057/9781137308733

is based upon evidence that can be tested and falsified, then a first step is formulating claims about fraud into hypotheses or assertions that can withstand empirical investigation. Given, that, a first claim or hypothesis could be: "Voter fraud is a significant factor affecting the outcomes of elections." How do we test this? First of course one would need to define terms such as fraud and significant. After that, the best way of course would be controlled experiments or other empirical techniques where evidence of fraud is gathered and examined. However, there are no real studies that do that, but what little evidence that does exist fails to support this proposition. Instead, as Minnite and Schultz point out, existing studies actually falsify this claim by revealing very little detected fraud (Minnite 2010: 57; Schultz 2008a: 501). In response, John Fund and Judge Richard Posner will argue that the current failure to have voter identification precludes that.

Given that the first proposition cannot be supported with the existing evidence, there is a fallback second claim: "Voter ID will demonstrate the extent of voter fraud." This is a claim capable of being falsified. Empirical testing of this claim would look to instances where voter ID has been instituted to see whether more fraud has been detected. Perhaps also one might look to states with voter ID versus none to see whether more fraud is detected. However the latter is not a good test because different jurisdictions might have different levels of preexisting fraud and comparing them may be the classic "comparing apples to oranges" problem.

But "before and after" (institution of photo ID) is generally a good way to determine levels of fraud within a jurisdiction. It speaks to how much fraud or attempted fraud there is in a jurisdiction by offering new data when it is easier to detect. However, thus far, the evidence does not support this claim. Instead, the lack of increased detection of fraud falsifies this assertion. Simply put—institution of new voter photo ID requirements has yet to produce increased evidence of fraud.

Yet there is another claim offered by those who believe voter fraud is rampant to account for the lack of evidence. This would be the assertion that: "Institution of voter ID and lack of increase of fraud is proof that such identification works." However, to test this statement, one needs a baseline of fraud from before the ID was instituted and then look to see whether it decreased as a result. Another way to phrase it would be that there must be some change in the incidence of fraud from before and after the voter ID was instituted to be able to make that claim.

DOI: 10.1057/9781137308733

Again, there is no evidence that would allow one to reach the conclusion that voter ID decreases fraud because there was little evidence to support its existence initially. For example, in Indiana, the State conceded in the legal challenge to its photo ID law that it did not have a record of in-person election fraud (*Indiana Democratic Party v. Rokita* 458 F.Supp.2d 775, 972 (D. Ind. 2006)). There was no fraud initially in Indiana and subsequent implementation of the ID requirements has failed to detect previously hidden fraud.

Have we resolved the problem and demonstrated that voter fraud does not exist? Not really. Those who believe fraud exists still will make the claim that it does. They will contend that the few instances we see are examples of larger populations and more extensive fraud. Is this a hasty generalization or a reasonable inductive conclusion? At this point those who believe voter fraud exists as a serious problem will fall to another argument, invoking analogies. Voter fraud will be paralleled or analogized to speeding or littering as Smith as Posner do.

Many claim that the current rate or detection of voter fraud underreports the real or actual existence of voter fraud that exists. To assert this they argue that successful prosecution or detection of voter fraud is similar to police citations of speeding. By that, only a fraction of all speeding actually is detected and cited. The same claim is made about littering. However, this analogy is misplaced.

First, as opposed to concluding that the few instances of voter fraud are proof that the current system of detection works to root out what little fraud there is, the opposite conclusion is reached. Thus, the few instances are proof of broader and more systematic fraud. However, no evidence or proof is offered to support reaching this conclusion as opposed to the claim that there actually is very little fraud. There has to be some basis for reaching the broader claim and not the conclusion that the few reported instances are proof that current systems work to detect and root out fraud. In other words, what is the evidence supporting this generalization or inference? None is really offered to suggest that the sample is indicative of a broader population. Instead, the sample could be good proof that there in fact is little fraud.

Second, the analogy to vehicular speeding is inapt. Speeding in a car is a continuous 24/7 activity that can occur anytime and anywhere. (The same is true about littering.) There is no single detection point or place where people can speed and therefore with an almost infinite number of cars driving along almost infinite roads, it is virtually impossible to

DOI: 10.1057/9781137308733

detect all instances of speeding. Thus, the few speed traps that are set up obviously detect and capture only a small spectrum of all speeding. Here, sampling makes sense as a way to infer to a broader population.

However, voting or voter fraud is a discrete activity. It can occur only at a specific point in time or place and in order to commit fraud one has to do it by going through the specific point—a voting booth. Thus, all instances of fraud must go through and exit a single detection point. To be successful, in-person fraud requires either a false registration, false signature, and tricking an election judge. To commit voter fraud one has to get past multiple detection points or check points. One can speed without ever crossing a detection point (speed trap).

The point here is that the analogy of voter fraud to speeding or littering, as Judge Posner and Brad Smith assert, is inapt. One can speed or litter almost anytime or anyplace. This is why detection is hard. The few instances detected and prosecuted are perhaps only a small sample of a larger pattern of speeding and littering that may exist. In addition, beyond detection and prosecution, other evidence, such as police using radar guns to detect speeders but not issuing a ticket, or anecdotal statements from drivers that they speed, may corroborate inferences that it is more prevalent than prosecution may suggest. With littering, proof can be found along roadsides and fields across America.

One can only vote in person in a finite number of places and within a finite time. To vote, especially in person, there are several steps and checkpoints in place. There is in 42 states voter registration before election day. This is one check. For all 50 states, in-person voting requires someone to show up, give a name to an election judge and generally sign a log with which there is a signature match. There may be other requirements too. What this means is that one has to go to a specific place to commit fraud and cross past numerous detection or check points before one can actually submit a fraudulent ballot. One does not simply have to speed past a law enforcement officer to violate a motor vehicle law.

Because of the finite opportunities to commit in-person voter fraud, the analogy to littering and speeding is lacking in foundation. Contrary to Posner and Smith, the analogy is not correct. Moreover, given the critical differences—especially the finite opportunities to commit in-person voter fraud—one has to ask again whether the few instances of detected fraud are indication that the system generally works to prevent fraud, or that they are indicative or more extensive illegality? Given the current checks in place, and given any other good evidence to the

DOI: 10.1057/9781137308733

contrary, it is impossible to conclude that these few instances of fraud are empirical support that much more fraud exists. Yes, there may perhaps be a few more instances undetected, but in general current research fails to support any contention that voter fraud is a serious problem in the United States that has affected the outcome of any election that would be remedied by voter identification at the polls. Yes there is fraud, fraud perhaps committed by election officials and perhaps fraud in absentee voting. And yes, there may be some in-person voter fraud too. But at least for the latter, its existence is largely a myth. There is no question that elections could be run better in America. But for the most part to assert that there are hoards of people clamoring to the polls to vote, when presidential turnouts are 55–60%, state races barely 50%, and local races range with turnouts of 5% to 30%, seems illogical. The bigger worry in the United States should not be about voter fraud but about the anemic voter turnout compared to other countries in Europe and elsewhere where significantly larger percentages of the population vote. Our poor voter turnout and laws aimed to limit voting raise serious and embarrassing questions about the quality and commitment of America to democracy.

Legislative term limits

Legislative term limits have deep roots in American politics. Dating back to the Anti-Federalists and their critique of the new constitution, advocates of term limits see in them important values, including the republican idea of rotation in office to produce citizen–legislators. Moreover, the saying "Throw the bums out" is an often repeated sentiment uttered during election time to express disgust or disappointment with elected officials who have overstayed their welcome.

Americans often believe that elected officials go off to Washington, D.C. or the state legislatures, cozy up to lobbyists or otherwise become detached from constituents back home. Elected officials thus sell out or get corrupted, or are bought and paid for, according to the sentiment of some voters, and it becomes difficult, if not impossible, to dislodge them from office. Thus these officials turn into the worst of all possible creatures—career politicians—looking out more for their own interests than those they serve. It of course does not help that stories populate the news with tales of lobbyist gifts and trips, lavish so-called fact-finding

DOI: 10.1057/9781137308733

trips paid for by lobbyists, political contributions from special interests, and then lucrative careers with organizations or firms that used to give them all these perks. The revolving door or public official to lobbyist bothers many. Now this anger over career politicians has boiled into frustration that Congress cannot get anything done. Gridlock is the first word of the day, with change, as Barack Obama making it his slogan of 2008, the second. Americans saying they hate politics as it is practiced today and think that by throwing the bums out things will change. Thus, one idea to remedy these problems is term limits. This translates into the policy myth that *legislative term limits will dismantle incumbent advantages, break their ties to special interests, and discourage career politicians.*

The frustration with special interest politics or the apparent corruption of career politicians led to the passage of legislative term limits in 21 states during the 1990s. The idea behind the movement for term limits is the belief that many of the ills affecting state legislative politics are rooted in career politicians who place self-interest above the public's interest, or who are otherwise embedded in lobbyist or special interest networks that make it impossible for them to legislate. Advocates also believed that term limits would change the type of people serving in legislatures, increase and promote competitive elections, and would change how work and power is allocated (Cain et al. (2006)). Some of the steam for term limits was taken out when several state legislatures imposed them on their congressional delegations only to have the Supreme Court in *U.S. Term Limits v. Thorton* 514 U.S. 779 (1995) declare them unconstitutional because states may not impose additional qualifications upon individuals running for office beyond those specified in the Constitution. Despite this ruling, term limits have been imposed at the state and local level, and in places like California they have led either to a shift of politicians out of the legislature and into a different office—such as Willie Brown from the legislature to Mayor of San Francisco—or to the retirement and replacement of some officeholders with others.

Have term limits lived up to their expectations as an important reform tool? At best, their reforms have fallen far short of their desired outcomes, while at worst they have had a negative impact on many aspects of legislative politics and power and, in some cases, have produced effects almost exactly counter to what was desired.

One of the earliest and most comprehensive studies on legislative term limits was an edited volume *The Test of Time* (Farmer et al. 2003). Written only within a couple of years after some of the first legislatures were

DOI: 10.1057/9781137308733

experiencing the initial impact of the term limits, the various articles in this volume concluded that the limits produced results which suggested "substantive, but mixed" results (5). For example, there was little evidence of a change in who ran for office, although there were modest gains in some states for women and minorities (6). Term limits seemed to have little impact on career incentives, with many of these individuals running for other offices or taking appointed political positions or becoming lobbyists (Powell 2003: 144). There was little evidence of increased competition for offices and, in fact, because career politicians continued to cycle their way through offices, there was some evidence that this phenomena (along with increased campaign costs for open seats) created new impediments for citizens contemplating a bid for office. Moreover, partisanship seemed to increase, knowledge among legislators decreased, and the ties to lobbyists and special interests that was supposed to break generally failed to materialize (Farmer et al. 2003). Finally, leadership skills in the legislature seemed weaker and the power of this branch of government overall diminished vis-a-vis the governor and executive branch. Perhaps the only real change that did occur in terms of what term limit advocates had hoped for was the production of more open seats.

Subsequent studies seemed to confirm these initial conclusions. Cain et al. (2006) found that while more seats were contested, the races were not necessarily more competitive. Term limits also did not seem to produce a partisan change of seats, more citizen responsiveness, or less bias (218). Sarbaugh-Thompson et al. (2002; 2004) found little, if any, evidence that term limits in Michigan produced increased voter turnout, weakened incumbency advantages, or increased more competitive elections. They also found that the elections under term limits generally cost more, did not necessarily make candidates less reliant upon special interest or lobbyist money, and that, in many cases, led to an increase in more self-financed wealthy candidates running. In short, they saw little evidence that term limits in Michigan attracted more citizen legislators (Sarbaugh-Thompson et al. 2004: 187) or that it diversified the legislature much from what was previously seen. Among the 11 promises they list that term limits advocates hoped their reforms would achieve, Sarbaugh-Thompson found only three of them were secured, with the remainder failing (191).

Kousser (2005) also concurred with many of the results noted above. However, in his research he examined how the increased professionalism

DOI: 10.1057/9781137308733

of legislatures (more pay or staff, for example) and term limits impacted this branch of government. His conclusion was that term limits offset any legislative improvements that were produced by professionalism. By that, terms limits resulted in a loss of legislative skills and institutional and policy knowledge, thereby shifting more expertise or knowledge to staff and lobbyists. He also found that generally term limits changed the knowledge and skill level of legislators and, most importantly, had a damaging impact both upon policy innovation and time lines for legislators (202). Term-limited legislators were less likely to look to policies that had longer time horizons for success, and generally less knowledgeable officeholders had less time to work on policies or draw upon their skills and experience to craft more innovative policies. Instead, they seemed more likely to follow what had been developed elsewhere, or relied upon ideas from staff or lobbyists. What one sees with term limits is that with significantly greater turnover of elected officials, more time had to be spent on learning curves to understand issues. It often takes years of experience to develop expertise in many complex areas. One can also contend that term limits have exacerbated and not mitigated partisanship and gridlock as fewer and fewer legislators have developed working relationships with one another or developed an affect or relationship with government agencies. In effect, term limits perhaps break important bonds or social capital critical to working with one another.

Kousser (2005), as well as other research, also reinforced much of what the initial research has tentatively concluded. Term limits strengthened the executive branch, especially with the budget, and failed to produce a new type of legislator. Research by Schaffner et al. (2004) indicated that term limits made redistricting more partisan. Carey et al. (2000) found little demographic change in term-limited legislatures, while Carroll and Jenkins (2001) found little evidence that female candidates benefitted from the reform. Carey et al. (2000) also noted increased partisanship, less cooperation in bicameral bodies, a shifting of power towards the governor, and a decrease in legislative knowledge and innovation. A 2006 study by the National Council of State Legislatures reached similar results. At the local level, there is no indication that term limits has produced different economic and distributive policies (McGlynn and Sylvester 2010). Similar trends have been noted by Dalle and Ricciuti (2011) in terms of social and welfare spending.

Other studies have noted a decrease in political accountability and competence in situations with terms limits, pointing to higher growth

DOI: 10.1057/9781137308733

and lower taxes in situations where governors can stand for reelection (Alt et al. 2011). There is also little evidence of increased competitiveness in congressional elections where state legislative term limits exist and presumably create situations where experienced legislators can run for higher office (Birkhead et al. 2010). As Weissert and Halperin (2007) point out, while the general public still seems to support term limits, those who follow it most closely dislike it. Some states, after passing term limits, have moved to undo them because they have failed to live up to their promises. Perhaps the most significant impact of term limits has been a boon to political science scholarship to study it (Mooney 2009).

To summarize, term limits as a "throw the bums out" strategy have failed to live up to their promise as a significant political reform and, in some cases, may actually weaken the very values its advocates wanted to promote. Term limits, if not a waste of money, certainly cannot be described as a successful reform but instead one that seems failed to solve the problems they were designed to address.

Conclusion

Voter photo identification is a great example of political myth, with term limits representing a great example of a failed public policy. Both were directed at solving a legitimate concern with the operations and performance of campaigns and elections in the United States. But as the evidence demonstrates, in-person voter fraud at the polls is not a significant problem in American elections today and one has a greater chance of being struck by lightning than it affecting the outcome of elections. The claim is not being made that some fraud does not exist or that there are problems with elections in the United States, but the type of difficulties that exist will not be solved by voter identification. Conversely, in all fairness, those who argue that voter ID will disenfranchise millions too seem short in offering evidence to support their claims. Thus, the debate over voter ID and its impact seems largely conjecture.

Additionally, entrenchment of politicians is a concern and incumbency advantage is certainly an issue affecting the competitiveness of elections. Yet again the evidence fails to show that term limits have really accomplished what its advocate urged. Term limits instead may lead to furthering strengthening of special interests and dependency of elected officials on players who are not accountable to the voters.

DOI: 10.1057/9781137308733

Taken together enactment of voter identification and term limits may actually produce less fair elections that deny individuals the right to vote for people whom they may wish to see elected. If some individuals are denied the right to vote based on alleged fraud, and some denied the right to serve, majority will is more poorly served. Finally, if incumbents are term limited out, the institutional memory and knowledge that they have is often lost, perhaps increasing the risk that more failed public policies will be enacted premised upon political myths that are false. In effect, one of the unintended consequences of term limits may be to exacerbate the chances that failed public policies and political myths were get enacted because we are increasingly producing public officials who lack the knowledge and experience to sort out fact from fiction.

DOI: 10.1057/9781137308733

Conclusion: Fool Me Twice, Shame on Me

Abstract: *Public officials repeatedly enact failed policies based upon political myths and not the best available facts or evidence at hand. The reasons for this are many, including the role of special interests, money in politics, and a general unwillingness or inability on the part of citizens and public officials to digest and process the type of information necessary to make good decisions. The consequence of all this is that the American political system repeatedly reenacts and implements policies that are perhaps doomed to fail from their inception. Contrary to the claims by many that states are laboratories of innovation, they instead are often failures in their ability to learn from previous mistakes.*

Keywords: States, federalism, special interest politics, innovation, money in politics, fact-based policy

Schultz, David. *American Politics in the Age of Ignorance: Why Lawmakers Choose Belief over Research*. New York: Palgrave Macmillan, 2013. DOI: 10.1057/9781137308733.

"Whereof one cannot speak, thereof one must remain silent."

Ludwig Wittgenstein, *Tractatus Logico-Philosophicus*

Why failed public policies and political myths never die

This book has highlighted several failed public policies and political myths that never seem to die. They are almost like zombies who live on in B movies, despite the evidence suggesting that they are flawed, badly designed, or in some cases, simply do not work or are untrue. They are often like fabled urban legends that live on across the country in pop culture. The goal of this book has not been to present original research regarding convention centers, taxes, or the host of other topics discussed in the various chapters. Instead it has sought to gather preexisting literature on the topics to prove a point—there already exists for policy makers to consider ample research that documents what we know and do not know about certain policies. Given the existence of this research, certain political myths continue to exist, leading to the recurrent enactment of failed public policies. This book has chosen to catalog just a few of these failed policies. What this book speaks to is a significant gap between what good social science research tells us versus the information elected officials and policymakers act upon. If the evidence suggests that some public policy ideas are myths or are shown to be defective based upon social science research, how can one explain their immortality? While it is not the purpose of this book to offer a detailed discussion of the causes, several theses are possible.

First, perhaps the simplest answer is that many elected officials, policy makers, and members of the public may be unaware that the policies do not work. It may also be that the lack of staff time and resources at the state and local level reinforce this ignorance. This is the argument advanced in Chapter 1. States are strapped for resources and often times instead of being laboratories of innovation they are simple copycats, simply reproducing policies that were previously adopted elsewhere, without asking or investigating how well they performed there. In addition, if the research on term limits is accurate, less experienced legislators might be more likely to repeat these failures simply because they lack institutional and policy memory to know any better.

DOI: 10.1057/9781137308733

Even though this book has potentially run roughshod over some of the nuances of the research regarding the different policies discussed, there is no question that many policy makers may well be unaware or unable to digest the various studies on welfare migration, economic development, or any of the other topics under discussion here. Furthermore, this is not a book indicting public officials for making simple but honest mistakes when enacting policies that they thought would work. The argument here is different. Given that many policy makers may rely upon almost a word of mouth in constructing policies, they simply may be outside the information loop when it comes to policy evaluation and knowledge about what does or does not work. Moreover, they may simply not be able to appreciate the differences or significance of what social scientists are arguing, or the latter may not be very good at communicating their thoughts and speaking to the broader public. Few policy makers or elected officials are trained as economists, sociologists, clinical psychologists, or even statisticians. They are either unaware or unable to process social science evidence or comprehend facts when presented to them.

But even more strongly, it may be that some public officials are simply negligent in doing their homework. If the purpose of committee hearings is fact finding and the gathering of information to make good policy, then there is an expectation that public officials should be making their decisions on the basis of the best available information that exists. If they are not doing that, or if they are willfully ignoring this information for other reasons such as personal or partisan gain, then this is a dereliction of their duties as public officials.

The policy process may also be limited by the anti-intellectual bias in America. Richard Hofstadter (1964) once noted an anti-intellectual strain in American politics and culture. There is a disdain for learning that views it as anti-democratic and elitist. The point here is that running as a populist often seems to run counter to running as someone who is well educated and able to digest complex data and then explain it to the public. Telling the public they are wrong or dismissing prejudice and folk wisdom (even if wrong) is difficult for politicians to do.

A second argument for the persistence of failed policies and myths is a belief that if it works in one place it will work in another, or that while it did not work somewhere else, this time or in this place it is different. There are two problems here. The first argument relies upon a false aggregation thesis. By that, something that works in Chicago should also work here. However, not every place is Chicago, and the novelty or scarcity of an attraction may make it a draw in a limited number of cities, but not one when the market is flooded with them. We saw this point discussed in the context of convention centers, for example. Conversely, policymakers, while acknowledging that a stadium plan did not work elsewhere, will argue that this time it is different because the sports subsidy now is embedded in, for example, a broader commercial revitalization project. Thus, unlike the failures of the past, this project learns from their mistakes and will work. Maybe the belief that this time it will be different is a reasonable mistake, but again, given the evidence of past failures, public officials should be more skeptical about how it will be different this time. There is the old folk line that insanity is doing the same thing over and over again will produce different results. Perhaps political insanity is re-enacting the same policies over and over again and expecting different results.

More cynically, there are also several reasons why failed public policies and political myths persist. Interest group politics, as well as the impact of money in politics, could account for why some policies endure despite evidence to the contrary. As Schultz (2002) and others have documented, states are increasingly facing strong pressures from interest groups and money in politics that distorts the policy process. Additionally, in the case of welfare migration and immigration, fear and prejudice may drive the topics. In situations, partisan or personal electoral politics may explain why elected officials push three strikes laws. For example, Fulton (2011) asserts that partisan politics prevents good fact-based policy. He notes how when California Governor Jerry Brown sought to eliminate an ineffective tax cut, Republicans in the state opposed it calling the closing of the program a tax increase. Partisan politics should not insulate failed policies, but sometimes it happens, especially when there is interest group or lobbyist support for them that pressure elected officials to let them be.

Here, despite whatever one may know intellectually, politically it may be pragmatic to push specific policies for personal gain. There are few incentives to respond to social science research and incorporate it into best practices for policy. Furthermore, and even more cynically, perhaps those individuals and groups who are most likely to be pressing many of these unsuccessful policy ideas are those who least support an activist government. Thus, while at the same time engaging in what economists call rent-seeking behavior they are also setting government up to fail. The result is that this tactic both reinforces the idea that the government is the problem, not the solution, and it feeds upon public cynicism toward it.

DOI: 10.1057/9781137308733

Another reason why some policies live on may be rooted in the narrow political orientations found within American culture. Given a basically pro-market orientation towards the economy, appeals to market incentives might well determine what types of economic solutions may be offered by political leaders and be considered acceptable by the public. For example, when Francois Mitterand was elected the Socialist President of France in 1981 he was asked whether he planned to nationalize a specific French car company. He replied no, asking why he would take over a company losing money. Instead, he wanted to take over businesses making money so that it could finance government programs. In the United States, nationalizing a business, especially a profitable one, would clearly cut against the grain of the ideology of many.

But there are two final reasons for the immortality of some policy ideas. First, perhaps politics and political choices are not about reason but passion. By that, David Hume (1980: 415), Murray Edelman (1985), and recent works by Frank (2005) and Westen (2007) may be correct— politics and policy making are not rational, but more symbolic and emotive. This means regardless of what research may suggest, policy ideas are driven by variables other than disinterested reason. Second, the persistence of often repeated failed policies may speak to Brandeis' assertion that states are laboratories of democracy. Perhaps they should not be so characterized. Instead, states may be more often than not described as displaying a lack of innovation. In reaching this conclusion, researchers almost need to invert the diffusion literature, asking not why or how states innovate, but why they mindlessly replicate policy mistakes and myths.

"Stupid is as stupid does." So said Forrest Gump of the motion picture by the same name, in referring to how stupid individuals do stupid things. While this book examined only a handful of failed public policies and other political myths, a host of others—including encouraging casinos and lotteries as tools of economic development, privatization of government services as a quick cost savings device, and the myth of government ineptitude—warrant exploration and demolition. Governments may not be inherently stupid, but oftentimes they pursue policies that fit that category.

This book has examined failed public policies and political myths within the context of the literature on state diffusion and innovation in order to raise several questions. First, it looked at the gap between political myth and social science research, asking how the political process

DOI: 10.1057/9781137308733

can be better informed when policy is made. It also queries to whether policy making should be data-driven. These two questions reflect the often contrasting perspectives of elected and appointed officials who see the world from different vantage points. While many would like to see budgets, policy, and laws reflect good social science evidence that is rational, others may say that all three of these items are political issues that reflect clashing ideologies and values. There is no reason to think that data should not drive the policy process; after all, this is what is taught in business schools and is preached among those who write all those *New York Times* business books best-sellers. If government is to be run more like a business then it too should draw upon good data and evidence to make policy. If, as noted earlier on in this book, the demand is to make government more effective, do more with less, or simply show results, we cannot continue to legislate failed policies premised upon political myths. If in fact the government is inevitably going to make policy, it should at least do so in a way that generates value for the tax-payer (Osborne and Hutchinson (2004)).

This book has asked lots of questions about state innovation and learning. While the diffusion literature has sought to understand how governments learn, this book has suggested that the innovation is less than meets the eye. States may adopt policies from elsewhere but how good of a job do they do in learning from the mistakes of others. It is not clear they do learn, raising questions about the laboratories of democracy label often pinned on to states. Instead, too much of what passes for policy is a recycling of failed ideas, making one wonder whether politics is simply living in the movies *Groundhog Day* or the *Truman Show*. For all of those who like to celebrate states rights, federalism, and the belief that more power should return to the state and local level, this book should give pause to the wisdom of thinking that these officials are any better at making policy than those at the federal level.

Finally, this book should not be read as a wholesale indictment of government or of democracy. This is not a diatribe that says government can never do anything right and therefore the solution is less government or destroy it. Government in America has accomplished a significant amount, ranging from putting a man on the Moon, winning several wars and the Cold War, helping find a cure for Polio, and so much more. The list is impressive and often overlooked. The Marshall Plan, the building of the interstate highway system, clean water, sewers, fluoridation, Head Start, the Tennessee Valley Authority, and countless other famous

DOI: 10.1057/9781137308733

and mundane activities demonstrate the capacity of governments to be successful and make meaningful differences in the lives of Americans. Yet despite these accomplishments, government can still improve. It can execute better if simply it does what seems to make sense—learn from the past and from the evidence to make future choices better informed.

Democracy is messy. American democracy is plagued by special interests, money, lobbyists, partisanship, and anger. These are just some of the factors that compromise the ability of the political process to move beyond repetition of failed policies and political myths. As the title of this book indicates, we seem to be living in an era of age of ignorance at all levels that seem to make it difficult for public officials to do the right thing and act upon what the evidence tells us. This is not a plea to say the social scientists have all the answers or that they ought to rule. Instead it is both an indictment on the part of social scientists that they have done such a poor job in communicating their research to a broader audience, and of elected officials and of a general public that seems unable to move beyond failed policies and myths when making decisions.

DOI: 10.1057/9781137308733

Bibliography

ABC News. 2011. "Michele Bachmann's HPV Vaccine Safety and 'Retardation' Comments Misleading, Doctors Say." http://abcnews.go.com/Health/ Wellness/michele-bachmanns-hpv-vaccine- safety-retardation-comments-misleading/ story?id=14516625#.T6lih8W_nlU (Site last visited on June 15, 2012).

Allard, Scott and Sheldon Danziger. 1997. "Welfare Migration and the Race to the Bottom: Empirical and Political Realities." Unpublished paper presented at 1997 annual meeting of the American Political Science Association annual convention, August 28–September 1, Chicago, Illinois.

Alt, James, Ethan Bueno de Mesquita, and Shanna Rose. 2011. "Disentangling Accountability and Competence in Elections: Evidence from U.S. Term Limits." *Journal of Politics*. vol. 73, no. 1, pp. 171–186.

Anderson, John E. and Robert W. Wassmer. 2000. *Bidding for Business: The Efficacy of Local Economic Development Incentives in a Metropolitan Area.* Kalamazoo, MI: W.E. Upjohn Institute for Employment Research.

Baade, Robert and Richard Dye. 1990. "The Impact of Stadiums and Professional Sports on Metropolitan Area Development." *Growth and Change* (spring), vol. 22, pp. 1–14.

Baade, Robert. 1994. "Stadiums, Sports and Economic Development: Assessing the Reality." Hearthland Policy study, no. 2. Chicago: Heartland Institute.

DOI: 10.1057/9781137308733

Bachrach, Peter, and Morton Baratz. 1962. "Two Faces of Power" *American Political Science Review* 56(December), pp. 947–952.

Bailey, Michael A. 2005. "Welfare and the Multifaceted Decision to Move." *American Political Science Review* (February), vol. 99, no. 1, pp. 125–35.

Baldo, Mariella. 1998. "AIDS and School Education." *World Health* (November), vol. 51, p. 22.

Balla, Steven J. 2001. "Interstate Professional Associations and the Diffusion of Policy Innovations." *American Politics Research*, vol. 29, no. 3, pp. 221–245.

Baltimore Sun. 2002. "Cash-Strapped Denver Aquarium about to Close," March 24, http://articles.baltimoresun.com/2002-03-24/news/0203240325_1_ocean-journey-aquarium-shedd

Bartik, Timothy J. 1991. *Who Benefits from State and Local Economic Development Policies?* Kalamazoo, MI: W.E. Upjohn Institute for Employment Research.

Bartlett, Bruce. 2010. "Bush Tax Cuts Had Little Positive Impact on Economy." *The Fiscal Times*, http://www.thefiscaltimes.com/Columns/2010/09/17/Bush-Tax-Cuts-No-Economic-Help.aspx#IcjjCx5XIfbuolxf.99 (Last viewed on August 3, 2012).

Baumgartner, Frank R. and Beth L. Leech. 1998. *Basic Interests: The Importance of Groups in Politics and in Political Science.* Princeton: Princeton University Press.

Bearman P.S., and Bruckner H. 2001. "Promising the Future: Virginity Pledges and First Intercourse." *American Journal of Sociology*, vol. 106, no. 4. pp. 859–912.

Belluck, Pam. 2012. "No Abortion Role Seen for Morning-After Pill." *New York Times* (June 6), A1.

Berenson, Alex. 2007. "Tax Breaks Used by Drug Makers Failed to Add Jobs as Advertised." *New York Times* (July 24), A1.

Bernstein, Mark F. 1998. "Sports Stadium Boondoggle." *Public Interest* vol. 132, pp. 45–57.

Berry, F.S. and W.D. Berry. 1990. "State Lottery Adoptions as Policy Innovations: An Event History Analysis." *American Political Science Review*, vol. 84, no. 2, pp. 395–415.

Bierschbach, Briana, 2012. "What's in the Final Stadium Bill?" *Saint Paul Legal Ledger*, May 14, p. 1.

Birkhead, Nathanie, Gabriel Uriarte, and William Bianco,. 2010. "The Impact of State Legislative Term Limits on the Competitiveness of

DOI: 10.1057/9781137308733

Congressional Elections." *American Politics Research*, vol. 38, no. 5, pp. 842–861.

Blake, John. 2012. "Return of the 'Welfare Queen.'" CNN.com, January 23, http://www.cnn.com/2012/01/23/politics/weflare-queen/index.html (site last visited on August 6, 2012).

Blanton, Dana. 2011. " Fox News Poll: 24 Percent Believe Obama Not Born in U.S." http://www.foxnews.com/politics/2011/04/07/fox-news-poll-24-percent-believe-obama-born/#ixzz1xrUIoTbk (Site last viewed on June 15, 2012).

Blotz, Timothy. 2011. "Michele Bachmann: Why Conservatives Believe Her: A Case of Belief-Based Reasoning on the State of the Union Response." Unpublished paper.

Boarnet, John, David A. Jaeger, and William T. Bogart. 1996. "Enterprise Zones and Employment: Evidence from New Jersey." *Journal of Urban Economics*, vol. 40, no. 2, pp. 198–215.

Bond, Shannon. 2011. "States Play Tax Credit Contest to Attract Jobs." *Financial Times* (September 26), p. 3.

Bound, John, David Jaeger, and Regina Baker. 1995. "Problems with Instrumental Variables Estimation when the Correlation between the Instruments and the Endogenous Explanatory Variable is Weak." *Journal of the American Statistical Association*, vol. 90, no. 430, pp. 443–450.

Bruckner H. and P.S. Bearman. 2005. "After the Promise: The STI Consequences of Adolescent Virginity Pledges." *Journal of Adolescent Health*, vol. 36, no. 4, pp. 271–278.

Bryce, James. 1889. *The American Commonwealth*, vol. 2. New York: Macmillan and Co.

Cain, Bruce, John Hanley, and Thad Kousser. 2006. "Term Limits: A Recipe for More Competition?" In Michael P. McDonald and John Samples (eds.) *The Marketplace of Democracy: Electoral Competition and American Politics*. Washington, DC: Brookings Institution Press, pp. 199–221.

California Budget Project. 2006. "New Study Overstates the Effectiveness of Enterprise Zones." *Budget Brief* (August).

Carey, John M., Richard G. Niemi, and Lynda W. Powell. 2000. *Term Limits in the State Legislatures*. Ann Arbor, MI: University of Michigan Press.

Carroll, Susan J. and Krista Jenkins. 2001. "Do Term Limits Help Women Get Elected?" *Social Science Quarterly*, vol. 82, no. 1 (March), pp. 197–202.

DOI: 10.1057/9781137308733

Center for Democracy and Election Management, American University. 2005. "Building Confidence in U.S. Elections: Report of the Commission on Federal Election Reform." Washington, DC

Chen, Elsa Y. 2008. "Close Impacts of 'Three Strikes and You're Out' on Crime Trends in California and Throughout the United States." *Journal of Contemporary Criminal Justice*, vol. 24, no. 4, pp. 345–370.

Chomsky, Aviva. 2007. *They Take Our Jobs! And 20 Other Myths About Immigration*. Boston: Beacon Press.

Citro, Constance F. and Michael, Robert T 1995. *Measuring Poverty: A New Approach*. Washington, DC: National Academy Press.

Coates, Dennis, and Brad R. Humphreys. 2000. "The Stadium Gambit and Local Economic Development." *Regulation*, vol. 23, no. 2, pp. 15–20.

Cobb, Roger W. and Elder, Charles D. 1972. *Participation in American Politics: The Dynamics of Agenda Building*. Boston: Allyn and Bacon.

Conkey, Christopher . 2006. "Attention, Voters: Have Your ID Ready." *Wall Street Journal* (October 31), D1.

Cooper, Michael. 2012. "Casino Boom Has States Looking to the Internet for Gambling Dollars." *New York Times* (August 3), A13.

Dahl, Robert A. 1971. *Polyarchy: Participation and Opposition*. New Haven, CT: Yale University Press.

Dahl, Robert A. 1979. *Who Governs? Democracy and Power in an American City*. New Haven, CT: Yale University Press.

Dahl, Robert A. 1976. *Democracy in the United States: Promise and Performance*. New Haven, CT: Yale University Press.

Dahl, Robert A. 1989. *Democracy and Its Critics*. New Haven, CT: Yale University Press.

Dailard, C. 2000. "Fueled by Campaign Promises, Drive Intensifies to Boost Abstinence-Only Education Funds." *The Guttmacher Report on Public Policy*, vol. 3, no. 2, pp. 1–2 & 12.

Dailard C. 2002. "Abstinence Promotion and Teen Family Planning: The Misguided Drive for Equal Funding." *The Guttmacher Report on Public Policy*, vol. 5, no. 1, pp. 1–3.

Dalle, Nogare and Robert Ricciuti. 2011. "Do Term Limits Affect Fiscal Policy Choices?" *European Journal of Political Economy*, vol. 27, no. 4, pp. 681–692.

Danielson, Michael N. 1997. *Home Team: Professional Sports and the American Metropolis*. Princeton: Princeton University Press.

DOI: 10.1057/9781137308733

Davis, Jonathan E. 1997. "The National Voter Registration Act of 1993: Debunking States' Rights Resistance and the Pretense of Voter Fraud,." *Temple Political & Civil Rights Law Review*, vol. 6, pp. 117–137.

De Jong, Gordon F, Deborah Roempke Graefe, and Tanja St Pierre. 2005. "Welfare Reform and Interstate Migration of Poor Families." *Demography*, vol. 42, no. 3, pp. 469–496.

De Tocqueville, Alexis. 1961. *Democracy in America*, vol. 1. Henry Reeve, trans. New York: Schocken Books.

Delaney, Kevin and Rick Eckstein. 2004. *Public Dollars, Private Stadiums: The Battle over Building Sports Stadiums*. New Brunswick, NJ: Rutgers University Press.

DelliCarpini, Michael X. and Scott Keeter 1989. *What Americans Don't Know About Politics and Why It Matters*. New Haven, CT: Yale University Press.

Dennis, Richard J. 1990. "The Economics of Legalizing Drugs." *Atlantic Monthly* (November), p. 126.

Downs, Anthony. 1972. "Up and Down with Ecology: The Issue-Attention Cycle." *Public Interest* (Summer), no. 28, pp. 38–50.

Eagleton Institute of Politics Center for Public Interest. 2005. "National Survey of Local Election Officials' Experiences with Provisional Voting." New Brunswick, NJ: Eagleton Institute of Politics Center for Public Interest.

Economist. 2012. "Evidence, Shmevidence." June 16, pp. 32–33.

Economist. 2012. "Bread, Circuses, and Leather Balls." May 19, pp. 36–37.

Edelman, Murray. 1985. *The Symbolic Use of Politics*. Bloomington, IL: University of Illinois Press.

Edmondson, Brad. 1996. "Life without Illegal Immigrants." *American Demographics*, vol. 18, no. 5, p. 1.

Edwards, L., Steinman, M., Arnold, K., and E. Hakanson, E. 1980. "Adolescent Pregnancy Prevention Services in High School Clinics." *Family Planning Perspectives*, vol. 12, pp. 6–14.

Eisinger, Peter. 2000. "The Politics of Bread and Circuses: Building the City for the Visitor Class." *Urban Affairs Review*, vol. 35, no. 3, pp. 316–333.

Elazar, Daniel J. 1984. *American Federalism: A View from the States*. New York: HarperCollins.

Farmer, Rick, Rausch, John David Jr., and Green, John C. 2003. *The Test of Time: Coping with Legislative Term Limits*. Lanham, MD: Lexington Books.

DOI: 10.1057/9781137308733

Feng, Xiu. 2008. "Professional Sports Facilities, Teams, Government Subsidies, and Economic Impact." In *The Business of Sports*, Brad R. Humphreys and Dennis R. Howard (eds). Westport, CT: Praeger Publishers, vol. 1: pp. 125–152.

Fernando, Mark. 2003. "The Late-Night Effect: Late-Night Television's Effect on the Perception of Political Figures." Master's Thesis, Georgetown University, May 1.

Field of Dreams. 1989. Directed by Phil Alden Robinson. Universal Studios.

Fisher, Peter S. and Alan Peters. 1997. "Tax and Spending Incentives and Enterprise Zones." The Effects or State and Local Public Policies on Economic Development Symposium, *New England Economic Review* (March/April), pp. 109–30.

Fitrakis, Robert, Steven Rosenfeld, and Harvey Wasserman. 2006. *What Happened in Ohio? A Documentary Record of Theft and Fraud in the 2004 Election*. New York: New Press.

Fitzgerald, Joan and Nancey Green Leigh. 2002. *Economic Revitalization: Cases and Strategies for City and Suburb*. Thousand Oaks, CA: Sage Publications.

Foley, Elise. 2011 "Obama Administration Sets Deportation Record." *Huffington Post*, October 18 http://www.huffingtonpost.com/2011/10/18/deportations-customs-remove-record-number_n_1018002.html (Last viewed on June 7 2012).

Ford, Larry R. 2003. *America's New Downtowns: Revitalization or Reinvention*. Baltimore, MD: The Johns Hopkins University Press.

Frank, Thomas. 2005. *What's the Matter with Kansas? How Conservatives Won the Heart of America*. New York: Holt Paperback.

Frankfort-Nachmias, Chava and David Nachmias. 2000. *Research Methods in the Social Sciences*. New York: St. Martin's Press.

Frey, W., Liaw, K., Xie Y., and Carlson M. 1995. *Interstate Migration of the U.S. Poverty Population: Immigration "Pushes" and Welfare Magnet "Pulls."* Research Report No. 95–331, University of Michigan Population Studies Center.

Fulton, William. 2011. "Tax Credit or Tax Cut?" *Governing* (July), pp. 22–23.

Fund, John. 2004. *Stealing Elections: How Voter Fraud Threatens Our Democracy*. New York: Encounter.

Fund, John. 2007. "Vote-Fraud Demagogues." *Wall Street Journal* (June 13), A19.

DOI: 10.1057/9781137308733

Furstenberg, Frank F. Jr., Lynne Maziarz Geitz, Julien O. Teitler, and Christopher C. Weiss. 1997. "Does Condom Availability Make a Difference? An Evaluation of Philadelphia's Health Resource Centers." *Family Planning Perspectives* (May–June) vol. 29, no. 3, pp. 123–128.

Gallup, George Gallup, Jr. 1993. *The Gallup Poll: Public Opinion 1993.*

Gallup, George Gallup, Jr. 1994. *The Gallup Poll: Public Opinion 1994.*

Giulietti, Corrado, Martin Guzi, Martin Kahanec, and Klaus F. Zimmermann. 2013. "Unemployment Benefits and Immigration: Evidence from the EU." *International Journal of Manpower.*vol. 34, no. 1/2 (also CEPR DP 8672; IZA DP 6075; 2011)

Giulietti, Corrado . 2012. "Welfare Migration." Bonn, Germany: Jackline Wahba Institute for the Study of Labor.

Giulietti, Corrado and Jackline Wahba. 2012. "Welfare Migration." SRRN Network. http://papers.ssrn.com/sol3/papers.cfm?abstract_id=2039636 (Site last viewed on October 8, 2012.)

Gold, Howard. 2012. "Evidence Mounts That Tax Cuts Don't Create Jobs." *Market Watch.* (June 8), http://www.marketwatch.com/story/its-time-to-bury-supply-side-economics-2012-06-08 (Site last accessed on August 7, 2012).

Goldthwaite, Dannagal. 2002. "Pinocchio v. Dumbo: Priming Candidate Caricature Attributes in Late-Night Comedy Programs in 2000 and the Moderating Effects of Political Knowledge." Paper presented at the 2002 Annual American Political Science Annual Convention, August 29–September 1.

Goodman, Josh. 2009. "Hotel Fever." *Governing* (December), pp. 27–29.

Gray, Virginia. 1994. "Competition, Emulation, and Policy Innovation." In L.C. Dodd and C. Jillson (eds.) *New Perspectives on American Politics.* Washington, DC: CQ Press, pp. 230–248.

Gray. Virginia. 1973. "Innovation in the States: A Diffusion Study." *American Political Science Review,* vol. 67, no. 4, pp. 1174–1185.

Greenbaum, Robert and John Engberg. 2000. "An Evaluation of State Enterprise Zone Policies," *Policy Studies* Review, vol. 17, no. 2/3, pp. 29–46.

Greenwald, Glenn. 2009. *Drug Decriminalization in Portugal: Lessons for Creating Fair and Successful Drug Policies.* Washington, DC: Cato Institute.

Hall, Jeremy L. 2007. "Informing State Economic Development Policy in the New Economy: A Theoretical Foundation and Empirical

DOI: 10.1057/9781137308733

Examination of State Innovation in the United States." *Public Administration Review* (July–August), pp. 630–645.

Hallfors, Denise and Shereen Khatapoush. 2004. "'Sending the Wrong Message': Did Medical Marijuana Legalization in California Change Attitudes about and Use of Marijuana?" *Journal of Drug Issues* (Fall 2004), vol. 34, no. 4, p. 751

Hamilton, Alexander, John Jay, and James Madison. 1937. *The Federalist*. New York: Modern Library.

Hamilton, Brady E. and Stephanie J. Ventura. 2012. "Birth Rates for U.S. Teenagers Reach Historic Lows for All Age and Ethnic Groups." NCHS Data Brief, no. 89 (April).

Hanson, R, and Heaveny, M. 1994. *Do Welfare Magnets Attract?* Institute for Research on Poverty, Discussion Paper No. 1028–94.

Harris, Maya. 2007. "Prison Vs. Education Spending Reveals California's Priorities" (May 29). http://www.sfgate.com/cgi-bin/article.cgi?f=/c/a/2007/05/29/EDGGTP3F291.DTL (site last visited on June 15, 2012).

Hissong, Rod. 2003. "The Efficacy of Local Economic Development Incentives." In Sammis B. White, Richard D. Bingham, and Edward W. Hill (eds), *Financing Economic Development in the 21st Century*. Armonk, NY: M.E. Sharpe, pp. 131–144.

History Musings 2011. "The Republican Debate at the Reagan Library." http://historymusings.wordpress.com/2011/09/07/campaign-buzz-september-7-2011-full-text-transcript-republican-presidential-debate-ronald-reagan-library-rick-perry-mitt-romney-steal-show/ (Site last visited on June 15, 2012).

Hobbes, Thomas. 1962 and 1977. *Leviathan*. New York: Macmillan Publishing.

Hofstadter, Richard. 1964. *Anti-Intellectualism in American Life*. New York: Knopf.

Hofstadter, Richard. 2008. *The Paranoid Style in American Politics*. New York: Vintage Books.

Hoppin, Jason. 2009. "House Republicans Target Welfare Benefits for New Residents." *St. Paul Pioneer Press* (January 22), B1.

Housing and Urban Development. 2001. *Interim Assessment of Empowerment Zones and Enterprise Communities (EC/EZ) Program: A Progress Report*. Washington, DC: Department of Housing and Urban Development.

Hume, David. 1980. *A Treatise of Human Nature*. New York: Oxford University Press.

DOI: 10.1057/9781137308733

Indiana Democratic Party v. Rokita. 2006. 458 F.Supp.2d 775 (D. Ind.)

Isaak, Alan C. 1985. *Scope and Methods of Political Science.* Fort Worth, TX: Harcourt College Publishers.

Iyengar, Radha. 2008. "I'd Rather Be Hanged for a Sheep than a Lamb: The Unintended Consequences of 'Three-strikes' Laws." http://www.nber.org/papers/w13784.pdf (Site last visited on June 15, 2012).

Jacobs, Jane. 1985. *Cities and the Wealth of Nations.* New York: Vintage Books.

Jacobs, Jane. 2002. *The Death and Life of Great American Cities.* New York: Random House.

Jacobson, Louis. 2010. "The Truth-O-Meter Report Card on Michele Bachmann." http://www.politifact.com/truth-o-meter/article/2010/sep/21/bachmann-and-truth-o-meter-collected-works/ (site last visited on June 15, 2012).

Jenkins, Sally, 2009. "Does Football Cost Too Much?" *Parade,* November 29, http://www.parade.com/news/2009/11/29-does-football-cost-too-much.html

Johnson, Arthur T. 1995. *Minor League Baseball and Economic Development.* Chicago: University of Illinois Press.

Jones, Charles O. 1977. *An Introduction to the Study of Public Policy.* North Scituate, MA: Duxbury Press.

Jones, Charles O. 1984. *An Introduction to the Study of Public Policy.* Belmont, CA: Brooke/Cole.

Kant, Immanuel. 1965. *Critique of Pure Reason.* New York: St. Martin's Press.

Key, V.O. 1967. *Politics, Parties, & Pressure Groups.* New York: Thomas Y. Crowell Company.

Keyssar, Alexander. 2000. *The Right to Vote: The Contested History of Democracy in the United States.* New York: Basic Books.

Kieschnick, Michael. 1981. *Taxes and Growth: Business Incentives and Economic Development.* Washington, DC: Council of State Planning Agencies.

Kieschnick, Michael. 1995. "The Effect of State and Local Taxes on Economic Development: A Meta-analysis." http://www.thefreelibrary.com/The+effect+of+state+and+local+taxes+on+economic+development%3a+a...-a017478992 (Site last visited June 12, 2012).

Kingdon, John W. 1995. *Agendas, Alternatives, and Public Policies.* New York: HarperCollins.

DOI: 10.1057/9781137308733

Kirby, D. 2001. *Emerging Answers: Research Findings on Programs to Reduce Teen Pregnancy.* Washington, DC: National Campaign to Prevent Teen Pregnancy.

Kirby, D., Resnik, M. D., B. Downes, T. Kocher, P. Gunderson, S. Pothoff, D. Zelterman, and R.W. Blum. 1993. "The Effects of School-Based Health Clinics in St. Paul upon School-Wide Birth Rates." *Family Planning Perspectives*, vol. 25, pp. 12–16.

Kirby, D., Waszak, C., and J. Ziegler. 1991. "Six School-Based Clinics: Their Reproductive Health Services and Impact on Sexual Behavior." *Family Planning Perspectives*, vol. 23, pp. 6–16.

Kirby, Douglas. 2002. "The Impact of Schools and School Programs upon Adolescent Sexual Behavior." *Journal of Sex Research* (February), vol. 39, pp. 27–34.

Kisker, E. E., Brown, R. S., and Hill, J. 1994. *Health Caring: Outcomes of the Robert Wood Johnson Foundation's School-based Adolescent Health Care Program.* Princeton, NJ: Robert Wood Johnson Foundation.

Kochbar, Rakesh. 2006. *Foreign-Born Workforce and Native-Born Employment.* Washington, D.C: Pew Hispanic Center.

Kolko, Jed and David Neumark. 2009. *Do California's Enterprise Zones Create Jobs?* San Francisco, CA: Public Policy Institute of California.

Kousser, Thad. 2005. *Term Limits and the Dismantling of State Legislative Professionalism.* New York: Cambridge University Press.

Kovandzic, Tomislav, John Sloan III, and Lynne Vieraitis, Lynne. 2008. "'Striking Out' as Crime Reduction Policy: The Impact of 'Three Strikes' Laws on Crime Rates in U.S. Cities." *Justice Quarterly*, vol. 21, no. 2, pp. 207–239.

Kübler-Ross, Elisabeth. 1973. *On Death and Dying.* New York: Routledge.

Leftin, Joshua and Kari Wolkwitz. 2010. "Trends in supplemental nutrition assistance program participation rates: 2001–2008." Washington, DC: Mathematica Policy Research, produced for the United States Department of Agriculture, Current Perspectives on SNAP Participation.

LeRoy, Greg. 2005. *The Great American Jobs Scam: Corporate Tax Dodging and the Myth of Job Creation.* San Francisco: Berrett-Koehler.

Levine, P. and Zimmerman, D. 1995. "An Empirical Analysis of the Welfare Magnet Debate using only the NLSY." *NBER Working Paper Series*, Paper No. 5264.

DOI: 10.1057/9781137308733

Lewis, Oscar. 1969. "Culture of Poverty". In Moynihan, Daniel P. (ed.) *On Understanding Poverty: Perspectives from the Social Sciences*. New York: Basic Books. pp. 187–220.

Lindblom, Charles E. and David Cohen. 1979. *Usable Knowledge: Social Science and Social Problem Solving*. New Haven, CT: Yale University Press.

Lindblom, Charles E. and Edward J. Woodhouse. 1992. *The Police Making Process*. New York: Prentice Hall.

Liptak, Adam, 2007. "Fear but Few Facts in Debate on Voter IDs." *New York Times* (September 24), A12.

Lipton, Eric. and Ian Urbina. 2007. "In 5-Year Effort, Scant Evidence of Voter Fraud." *New York Times* (April 12), A1.

Long, Larry. 1988. *Migration and Residential Mobility in the United States*. New York: Russell Sage Foundation.

Lowi, Theodore J. 1969. *The End of Liberalism*. New York: W.W. Norton & Company, Inc.

Luttbeg, Norman. 2005. *Comparing the States and Communities: Politics, Government, and Policy in the United* States. Peosta, IA: Eddie Bowers Publishing.

Malizia, Emil E. and Edward J. Feser. 1999. *Understanding Local Economic Development*. New Brunswick, NJ: Center for Urban Policy Research.

Markusen, Ann and Amanda Johnson. 2006. *Artists' Centers: Evolution and Impact on Careers, Neighborhoods, and Economies*. Minneapolis, MN: Project on Regional and Industrial Economics, University of Minnesota: Part I.

Marshall, Thurgood. 1987. "Remarks at the Annual Seminar of the San Francisco Patent and Trademark Law Association."

Martinez, G., Copen, C.E. and Abma J.C. 2011. "Teenagers in the United States: Sexual Activity, Contraceptive Use, and Childbearing, 2006–2010 National Survey of Family Growth." National Center for Health Statistics. *Vital Health Statistics*, vol. 23, no. 31.

Mauer, Marc. 2010. "The Impact of Mandatory Minimum Penalties in Federal Sentencing." *Judicature* (July–August), vol. 94, no. 1, pp. 6–8, 40.

McConnell, Grant. 1966. *Private Power and American Democracy*. New York: Alfred A. Knopf.

McGlynn, Adam J. and Dari E. Sylvester. 2010. "Assessing the Effects of Municipal Term Limits on Fiscal Policy in U.S. Cities." *State and Local Government Review*. vol. 42, no. 2: 118–132.

DOI: 10.1057/9781137308733

McKean, Lisa. 2002. "Access to Income Supports for Working Families In Chicago – Executive Summary." Chicago, IL: Center for Impact Research.

McKinnish, Terra . 2006. "Welfare-Induced Migration at State Borders: New Evidence from Micro-Data." http://stripe.colorado. edu/~mckinnis/newmigo83006.pdf (site last visited on June 15, 2012).

McMurry, Martha. 2000. *Minnesota Migrants: A 2000 Public Use Microdata Sample Portrait*. St. Paul, MN: Minnesota State Demographic Center.

Miller, Warren E. and J. Merrill Shanks, 1996. *The New American Voter*. Cambridge: Harvard University Press.

Minnesota Planning. 1994. "AWelfare Migrants Add to Minnesota's Rolls." St. Paul, MN: Minnesota Planning.

Minnite, Lorraine C. 2010. *The Myth of Voter Fraud*. Ithaca, New York: Cornell University Press.

Minnite, Lorraine C. 2007a: *The Politics of Voter Fraud*. http:// projectvote.org/fileadmin/ProjectVote/Publications/Politics_of_ Voter_Fraud_Final.pdf. (Site last visited on June 14, 2012).

Minnite, Lorraine, C. 2007b. "An Analysis of Voter Fraud in the U.S." http://www.demos.org/pubs/analysis_voter_fraud.pdf (Site last viewed on June 15, 2012).

Mintrom, Michael. 1997. "Policy Entrepreneurs and the Diffusion of Innovation." *American Journal of Political Science*, vol. 41, no. 3., pp. 738–770.

Mooney, Christopher Z. 2009. "Term Limits as a Boon to Legislative Scholarship: A Review." *State Politics & Policy Quarterly*, vol. 9, no. 2 pp. 204–228.

Mooney, Christopher. 2012. *The Republican Brain: The Science of Why They Deny Science—and Reality*. Hoboken, NJ: Wiley.

Mooney, Christopher. 2006. *The Republican War on Science*. New York: Basic Books.

Moynihan, Daniel Patrick. 1969. *Maximum Feasible Misunderstanding: Community Action in the War on Poverty*. New York: The Free Press.

Nadadur, Ramanujan. 2009. "Illegal Immigration: A Positive Economic Contribution to the United States." *Journal of Ethnic & Migration Studies*, vol. 35, no. 6, pp. 1037–1052.

National Academy of Sciences. 1997. *The New Americans: Economic, Demographic, and Fiscal Effects of Immigration*. Washington, DC: National Academy of Science.

DOI: 10.1057/9781137308733

National Council of State Legislatures. 2006. *Coping with Term Limits: A Practical Guide.* Washington, D.C: National Council of State Legislatures.

Newcomer, S., Duggan, A., and Toczek, M. 1996. "Do School-Based Clinics Influence Adolescent Birth Rates?" In A. Mundigo (ed.), *Reproductive Health: Programme and Policy Changes Post-Cairo.* Belgium: IUSSP.

Noll, Roger and Andrew Zimbalist. 1997. *Sports, Jobs, and Taxes: The Economic Impact of Sports Teams.* Washington, DC: Brookings.

Oettinger. Gerald S. 1999. "The Effects of Sex Education on Teen Sexual Activity and Teen Pregnancy." *Journal of Political Economy* (June), vol. 107, p. 606.

Office for Democratic Institutions and Human Rights. 2007. "United States of America Mid-term Congressional Elections 7 November 2006." Warsaw: Office for Democratic Institutions and Human Rights.

Office of the Legislative Auditor. 1987. *Aid to Families with Dependent Children.* St. Paul, MN: State of Minnesota.

Office of the Legislative Auditor. 2000. *Welfare Reform.* St. Paul, MN: State of Minnesota.

Office of Legislative Auditor. 2008. *JOBZ Program.* St. Paul, MN: State of Minnesota.

Office of the President. 2005. *Economic Report of the President: 2005.* Washington, DC: Government Printing Office.

Orrenius, Pia M. and Madeline Zavodny. 2012. "The Economic Consequences of Amnesty for Unauthorized Immigrants." *CATO Journal*, vol. 32, no. 1, pp. 85–106.

Osborne, David and Peter Hutchinson. 2004. *The Price of Government: Getting the Results We Need in an Age of Permanent Fiscal Crisis..* New York: Basic Books.

Overton, Spencer. 2007. "Voter Identification." 105 *Michigan Law Review* 631–682.

Parent, Dale Parent. 1997. "Key Legislative Issues in Criminal Justice: Mandatory Sentencing." *National Institute of Justice: Research in Action* (January), pp. 1–2.

Parker, Robert Nash. 2012. "Worse Policy After Bad: How and Why California's 'Three Strikes' is a Complete Failure as Crime and Economic Policy, and What to Do About Either." *California Journal of Politics and Policy.*pp. 1–26, ISSN (Online) 1944-4370, DOI: 10.1515/cjpp-2012-0008, July.

DOI: 10.1057/9781137308733

Peters, Alan and Peter Fisher. 2003. "Enterprise Zones: How Effective Are They?" In Sammis B. White, Richard D. Bingham, and Edward W. Hill (eds), *Financing Economic Development in the 21st Century*. Armonk, NY: M.E. Sharpe, pp. 113–130.

Pew Center on the States. 2012. *Time Served: The High Cost, Low Returns of Longer Prison Terms*. Washington, D.C: Pew Center on the States.

Pew Research Center for the People & the Press. 2007. "Public Knowledge of Current Affairs Little Changed by News and Information Revolutions: What Americans Know: 1989–2007." April 15.

Pew Research Center. 2010. "Growing Number of Americans Say Obama Is a Muslim." http://pewresearch.org/pubs/1701/poll-obama-muslim-christian-church-out-of-politics-political-leaders-religious (Site last visited on June 15, 2012).

Pleck, Joseph H. 1992. "The Association of AIDS Education and Sex Education with Sexual Behavior and Condom Use Among Teenage Men." *Family Planning Perspectives* (May–June), vol. 24, no. 3, pp. 100–107.

Politico 2009. "58 percent of GOP Not Sure/Doubt Obama Born in us." http://www.politico.com/blogs/glennthrush/0709/58_of_GOP_not_suredont_beleive_Obama_born_in_US.html (Site last visited on June 15, 2012).

Pomper, Gerald M. 2001. "The Presidential Election." In Gerald M. Pomper (ed.) *The Election of 2000: Reports and Interpretations*. New York: Chatham House Publishers, pp. 125–155.

Popper, Karl. 1959. *The Logic of Scientific Discovery*. London: Hutchinson & Co.

Porter, Eduardo. 2005. "Not on the Radar: Illegal Immigrants Are Bolstering Social Security." *Generations*, vol. 29, no. 1, pp. 100–102.

Powell, Richard C. 2003. "The Unintended Effects of Term Limits on the Career Paths of State Legislators." In Farmer, Rick, Rausch, John David Jr., and Green, John C. (eds.) *The Test of Time: Coping with Legislative Term Limits*. Lanham, MD: Lexington Books, pp. 133–146.

Pressman, Jeffrey and Aaron Wildavsky. 1973. *Implementation*. Berkeley, CA: University of California Press.

Putnam, Robert. 2000. *Bowling Alone: The Collapse and Revival of American Community*. New York: Simon & Schuster.

Ramirez, Juan and William D. Crano. 2003. "Deterrence and Incapacitation: An Interrupted Time-Series Analysis of California's

DOI: 10.1057/9781137308733

Three-Strikes Law." *Journal of Applied Social Psychology*, vol. 33, no. 1, pp. 110–144.

Rappaport, Jordan and Chad Wilkerson. 2001. *What Are the Benefits of Hosting a Major League Sports Franchise?* Federal Reserve Bank of Kansas City, Economic Review, First Quarter, pp. 55–86.

Rasmussen Reports. 2011. *75% Support Showing Photo ID at The Polls.* http://www.rasmussenreports. com/public_content/politics/general_politics/ june_2011/75_support_showing_photo_id_at_the_polls

Rein, Martin. 1976. *Social Science and Public Policy.* New York: Penguin Books.

Reusse, Patrick. 2012. "Quite a Bonanza for Our Stadium Martyr," Zygi, May 11, http://www.1500espn.com/sportswire/ Reusse_Quite_a_bonanza_for_our_stadium_martyr_Zygi051112.

Rich, Wilbur C. 2000. *The Economics and Politics of Sports Facilities.* Westport, CT: Quorum Books.

Rivlin, Alice. 1971. *Systematic Thinking for Social Action.* Washington, DC: Brookings Institution.

Rosenthal, Alan. 1998. *The Decline of Representative Democracy: Process, Participation, and Power in State Legislatures.* Washington, DC: CQ Press.

Rosentraub, Mark S. 2008. "Sports Facilities and Urban Redevelopment: Private and Public Benefits and a Prescription for a Healthier Future." In Brad R. Humphreys and Dennis R. Howard (eds), *The Business of Sports.* Westport, CT: Praeger Publishers, vol. 3, pp. 57–80.

Rosentraub, Mark S. 2010. *Major League Winners: Using Sports and Cultural Centers as Tools for Economic Development.* New York: CRC Press.

Rosentraub, Mark. 1997. *Major League Losers: The Real Cost of Sports and Who's Paying for It.* New York: Basic Books.

Rousseau, Jean-Jacques. 1977. *The Social Contract.* Maurice Cranston, trans. New York: Penguin Books.

Ryan Lee Teten. 2011–12. "Mouthpiece of the Liberal Left? Jon Stewart and The Daily Show's 'Real' Coverage of Election 2008." *Public Integrity*, vol. 14, no. 1, pp. 67–84.

Samuelson, Paul and William Nordhaus. 2005. *Macroeconomics.* Columbus, OH: McGraw-Hill.

Sanders, Heywood T. 2002. "Convention Myths and Markets: A Critical Review of Convention Center Feasibility Studies." *Economic Development Quarterly*, vol. 16, no. 3, pp. 195–210.

DOI: 10.1057/9781137308733

Sanders, Heywood T. 1998. "Convention Center Follies." *Public Interest* (Summer), no. 132, pp. 58–73.

Sarbaugh-Thompson, Marjorie, Lyke Thompson, Lisa Marckini, John Strate, Richard C. Elling, and Charles D. Elder 2002. "Term Limits and Campaign Funding in Michigan: More Money, More Candidates, More Wealth." In David Schultz (ed.) *Money, Politics, and Campaign Finance Reform Law in the States.* Durham, NC: Carolina Academic Press, pp. 311–348.

Sarbaugh-Thompson, Marjorie, Lyke Thompson, Charles D. Elder, John Strate, and Richard C. Elling 2004. *The Political and Institutional Effects of Term Limits.* New York: Palgrave Macmillan.

Satcher, David, 2001. *The Surgeon General's Call to Action to Promote Sexual Health and Responsible Sexual Behavior.* Office of the Surgeon General. http://www.surgeongeneral.gov/library/sexualhealth/call. htm (Site last visited on July 25, 2007).

Schafer, John R. 1999. "The Deterrent Effect of Three Strikes Law." *FBI Law Enforcement Bulletin.* http://findarticles.com/p/articles/ mi_m2194/is_4_68/ai_54636132/?tag=content;col1 (site last visited on June 15, 2012).

Schaffner, Brian F., Wagner, Michael W.S., and Winburn, Jonathan. 2004. "Incumbents Out, Party In? Term Limits and Partisan Redistricting in State Legislatures." *State Politics & Policy Quarterly,* vol. 4, no. 4, pp. 396–414.

Schattschneider, E.E. 1960. *The Semi-Sovereign People: A Realist's View of Democracy in America.* New York: Holt, Rinehart and Winston.

Schattschneider, E.E. 1975. *The Semi-Sovereign People: a Realist's View of Democracy in America.* Hinsdale, IL: Wadsworth Publishing.

Scher, Richard K. 2011. *The Politics of Disenfranchisement: Why Is It So Hard to Vote In America?* Armonk, NY: M.E. Sharpe.

Schmenner, Roger W. *Making Business Location Decisions.* Englewood Cliffs, NJ: Prentice-Hall, 1982.

Schrag, Peter. 2004. *Paradise Lost: California's Experience, America's Future.* Berkeley: University of California Press.

Schram, Sandford, Lawrence Nitz, and Gary Krueger. 1998. "Without Cause or Effect: Reconsidering Welfare Migration as a Policy Problem." *American Journal of Political Science,* vol. 42, no. 1, pp. 210–230.

Schultz, David. 1993. "Rethinking Drug Criminalization Policies." *Texas Tech Law Review,* vol. 25, pp. 151–171.

DOI: 10.1057/9781137308733

Schultz, David. 1998. "State Tax Commuters: Classifications and Estimates." *15 State Tax Notes*, p. 355.

Schultz, David. 2000a. "No Joy in Mudville Tonight: Impact of 'Three Strike' Laws on State and Federal Corrections Policy, Resources, and Crime Control." *9 Cornell Journal of Law and Public Policy 557*.

Schultz, David. 2000b. "State Taxation of Interstate Commuters: Constitutional Doctrine in Search of Empirical Analysis." *16 Touro Law Review 435*.

Schultz, David. 2007. Email conversation with Tom Gillaspy.

Schultz, David. 2008a. "Less than Fundamental: The Myth of Voter Fraud and the Coming of the Second Great Disenfranchisement." *William Mitchell Law Review 34*: 484–532.

Schultz, David. 2008b. "Lies, Damn Lies, and Voter IDs: The Fraud of Voter Fraud." *Harvard Law & Policy Review On-line 1*: 1–8. http://hlpronline.com/2008/03/lies-damn-lies-and-voter-ids-the-fraud-of-voter-fraud/

Seckel, Al. 1986. *Bertrand Russell on God and Religion*. Amherst, NY: Prometheus Books.

Shenkman, Rick. 2009. *Just How Stupid Are We? Facing the Truth About the American Voter*. New York: Basic Books.

Sherman, Lawrence W. 1983. "Patrol Strategies for Police." In James Q. Wilson (ed.), *Crime and Public Policy 145–163*. New Brunswick, NJ: Transaction.

Shierholz, Heidi. 2010. *Immigration and Wages: Methodological Advancements Confirm Modest Gains for Workers*. Washington, DC: Electronic Policy Institute.

Shipman, Charles R. and Craig Volden. 2006. "Bottom-Up Federalism: The Diffusion of Antismoking Policies from U.S. Cities to States." *American Journal of Political Science*, vol. 50, no. 4, pp. 825–843.

Shropshire, Kenneth. 1995. *The Sports Franchise Game*. Philadelphia: University of Pennsylvania Press.

Siegfried, John and Andrew Zimbalist. 2000. "The Economics of Sports Facilities and Their Communities." *Journal of Economic Perspectives* (Summer), vol. 14, no. 3, pp. 95–114.

Simon, Herbert. 1997. *Administrative Behavior*. New York: Free Press.

Singh, Simon. 2004. *Big Bang: The Most Important Scientific Discovery of All Time and Why You Need to Know About It*. New York: Harper Perennial.

Smith, Adam. 1937. *An Inquiry Into the Nature and Causes of the Wealth of Nations*. New York: P.F. Collier & Son.

DOI: 10.1057/9781137308733

Smith, Bradley. 2010. Election Law Listserv. Available at http://mailman. lls.edu/pipermail/election-law/2010-October/023420.html (Last viewed on August 9, 2012).

Snell, Ronald. 1998. *A Review of State Economic Development Policy.* Denver, CO: National Council of State Legislatures.

Steffens, Lincoln. 2011. *The Shame of the Cities.* Toronto: University of Toronto Libraries.

Stein, Rob. 2010. "Abstinence-Only Programs Might Work, Study Says." *Washington Post.* February 2. http://www.washingtonpost.com/ wp-dyn/content/article/2010/02/01/AR2010020102628.html (Site Last viewed on October 8, 2012.)

Stephenson, Jr., Donald Grier. 2004. *The Right to Vote: Rights and Liberties Under the Law.* Santa Barbara: ABC-CLIO.

Stone, Deborah. 2001. *Policy Paradox: The Art of Political Decision Making.* New York: W.W. Norton & Company.

Story, Sharone. 2011. "The Elderly in Prison: A Growing Concern." Corrections.com (May 16). http://www.corrections.com/news/ article/28550-the-elderly-in-prison-a-growing-concern (site last visited on June 15, 2012)

Sulak, Patricia J. , Sara J. Herbelin, Thomas J. Kuehl, and Dee Dee A. Fix. 2006. "Impact of An Adolescent Sex Education Program That Was Implemented by An Academic Medical Center." *American Journal of Obstetrics and Gynecology* (July), vol. 195, pp. 78–85.

Teodoro, Manuel P. 2007. "Bureaucratic Career Mobility and Policy Innovation." Unpublished paper prepared for presentation at the Gerald R. Ford Fellows' Reunion Conference, Ann Arbor, MI (May 12).

Think Progress Justice. 2012. "California Spends Six Times More On Prison Inmates Than On College Students." http://thinkprogress. org/justice/2012/04/05/458148/california-spends-six-times-more- on-prison-inmates-than-on-college-students/?mobile=nc (site last visited on June 7, 2012).

Tracy, Dan. 2005. "Public Price: Convention Center Expansion Falls Short of Expectations for Area-Wide Profitability." *IRE Journal* (September–October).

Truman, David B. 1971. *The Governmental Process: Political Interests and Public Opinion.* New   York: Alfred A. Knopf.

Trumpbour, Robert C. 2007. *The New Cathedrals: Politics and Media in the History of Stadium Construction.* Syracuse, NY: Syracuse University Press.

DOI: 10.1057/9781137308733

Tufte, Edward. 1974. *Data Analysis for Politics and Policy*. Englewood Cliffs, NJ: Prentice-Hall, Inc.

U.S. Elections Assistance Commission, The Impact of the National Voter Registration Act of 1993 on the Administration of Elections for Federal Office 2005–2006: A Report to the 110th Congress (June 30, 2007), http://projectvote.org/fileadmin/ProjectVote/Publications/EAC_NVRArpt2006.pdf

U.S. Elections Assistance Commission. 2006. "Election Crimes: An Initial Review and Recommendations for Future Study." Washington, DC: U.S. Elections Assistance Commission.

United States Senate Republican Policy Committee. 2005. "Putting an End to Voter Fraud." Washington, DC: United States Senate Republican Policy Committee.

Van Horn, Carl E. 2006. "Power, Politics, and Public Policy in the States." In Carl E. Van Horn (ed.), *The State of the States*, Washington, DC: CQ Press, pp. 1–13.

Vitiello, Michael. 2002. "Three Strikes Laws." *Human Rights*, vol. 29, no. 2, pp. 3–6.

Walker, Jack. 1969. "The Diffusion of Innovations Among the American States," *American Political Science Review*, vol. 63, no. 2, pp. 880–899.

Walker, James. 1994. *Migration Among Low-Income Households: Helping the Witch Doctors Reach Consensus*. Institute for Research on Poverty, Discussion Paper No. 1031–94.

Wasylenko, Michael. 1997. "Taxation and Economic Development: The State of the Economic Literature." *State Tax Notes* (June 23), pp. 1883–1895.

Weiser, Wendy R. and Lawrence Norden. 2011. *Voting Law Changes in 2012*. New York: Brennan Center for Justice. http://brennan.3cdn.net/9c0a034a4b3c68a2af_9hm6bj6do.pdf

Weiser, Wendy. 2005. Response to the Report of the 2005 Commission on Federal Election Reform. New York: Brennan Center.

Weissert, Carol and Karen Halperin. 2007. "The Paradox of Term Limit Support." *Political Research Quarterly*, vol. 60, no. 3, pp. 516–530.

Welfare Law Center. 1996. *Welfare Myths: Fact or Fiction? Exploring the Truth About Welfare*. New York: Center on Social Welfare Policy and Law.

Wellings, K., J. Wadsworth, A.M. Johnson, J. Field, L. Whitaker, and B. Field. 1995. "Provision of Sex Education and Early Sexual Experience: The Relation Examined." *British Medical Journal*, (August 12), vol. 311, no. 7002, pp. 417–421.

DOI: 10.1057/9781137308733

Westen, Drew. 2007. *The Political Brain: The Role of Emotion in Deciding the Fate of the Nation*. New York: Public Affairs.

White, Sammis B., Richard D. Bingham, and Edward W. Hill. 2003. *Financing Economic Development in the 21st Century*. Armonk, NY: M.E. Sharpe.

Wilson, James Q. 1983. *Thinking about Crime*. New York: Vintage Books.

Wilson, William Julius. 1997. *When Work Disappears: The World of the New Urban Poor*. New York: Vintage.

Wilson, Woodrow. 1887. "The Study of Administration." *Political Science Quarterly* (June), p. 2.

Wittgenstein, Ludwig. 1983. *Tractatus Logico-Philosophicus*. Boston: Routledge & Kegan Paul, Ltd.

Wong, Melanie. 2012. "'Every Day I'm Crumblin': ASCE's Report Card for the Nation's Infrastructure." http://sciencewonks.com/2012/every-day-im-crumblin-asces-report-card-for-the-nations-infrastructure/ (Site last visited June 12, 2012).

Woodward, C. Vann. 1974. *The Strange Career of Jim Crow*. New York: Oxford University Press.

Wyckoff, Paul Gary. 2009. *Policy & Evidence in a Partisan Age*. Princeton: Princeton University Press.

Wymelenberg, Suzanne. 1990. *Science and Babies: Private Decisions, Public Dilemmas*. Washington, DC: National Academy Press.

Zabin, L. S., M.B. Hirsh, E.A. Smith, R. Street, R., and J.B. Hardy. 1986. "Evaluation of a Pregnancy Prevention Program for Urban Teenagers." *Family Planning Perspectives*, vol. 18, pp. 119–126.

Zakaria, Fareed. 2012. "Incarceration Nation." Time Magazine. March 25. http://fareedzakaria.com/2012/03/25/incarceration-nation/ (Site last visited on Ocober 8, 2012.)

Zedlewski, Sheila R. 2002. "Left Behind Or Staying Away? Eligible Parents Who Remain Off tanf." *New Federalism, Series B., No. B-51*, Washington, DC: The Urban Institute.

Ziegler, Harmon. 1964. *Interest Groups in American Society*. Englewood Cliffs, NJ: Prentice-Hall, Inc.

Zimmerman, Dennis. 1996. "Tax-Exempt Bonds and the Economics of Professional Sports Stadiums." Washington, DC: Congressional Research Services.

Zimring, Franklin E. and Gordon Hawkins. 1997. *Incapacitation: Penal Confinement and the Restraint of Crime*. New York: Oxford University Press.

DOI: 10.1057/9781137308733

Index

DOI: 10.1057/9781137308733

DOI: 10.1057/9781137308733

DOI: 10.1057/9781137308733

DOI: 10.1057/9781137308733

DOI: 10.1057/9781137308733

CPSIA information can be obtained at www.ICGtesting.com
Printed in the USA
LVOW06*2109310813

350453LV00005B/61/P